NEW ON THE JOB

A SCHOOL LIBRARY MEDIA SPECIALIST'S GUIDE TO SUCCESS

Ruth Toor and
Hilda K. Weisburg

AMERICAN LIBRARY ASSOCIATION

Chicago   2007

While extensive effort has gone into ensuring the reliability of information appearing in this book, the publisher makes no warranty, express or implied, on the accuracy or reliability of the information, and does not assume and hereby disclaims any liability to any person for any loss or damage caused by errors or omissions in this publication.

Composition in Berkeley and Avant Garde using InDesign for the PC.

Printed on 50-pound white offset, a pH-neutral paper stock, and bound in 10-point cover stock by McNaughton & Gunn.

The paper used in this publication meets the minimum requirements of American National Standard for Information Sciences—Permanence of Paper for Printed Library Materials, ANSI Z39.48-1992. ∞

Library of Congress Cataloging-in-Publication Data

Toor, Ruth, 1933–
    New on the job : a school library media specialist's guide to success /
Ruth Toor, Hilda K. Weisburg.
        p.   cm.
    Includes bibliographical references and index.
    ISBN-10: 0-8389-0924-8 (alk. paper)
    ISBN-13: 978-0-8389-0924-9 (alk. paper)
    1. School librarians—United States—Handbooks, manuals, etc.
2. Instructional materials personnel—United States—Handbooks, manuals,
etc. 3. School libraries—United States—Handbooks, manuals, etc.
4. Instructional materials centers—United States—Handbooks, manuals,
etc. 5. Library science—Vocational guidance—United States.   I. Weisburg,
Hilda K., 1942–   II. Title.
    Z682.4.S34T66 2007
    027.8—dc22   2006021124

ISBN-10: 0-8389-0924-8
ISBN-13: 978-0-8389-0924-9

Printed in the United States of America

11   10   09   08   07   5   4   3   2   1

To our grandchildren, who have brought
great joy into our lives

> *Catherine and Joshua Toor*
> *Skye and Erik Toor*
>
> *Benjamin and Matthew Weisburg*
> *Ethan and Max Gofstein*

CONTENTS

INTRODUCTION

New on the Job: A School Library Media Specialist's Guide to Success will help you hit the ground running when you walk into a new school. Whether this is your first job or you have already been in the field for a few years but are changing your building level or starting in another district, our total of sixty years of experience successfully managing library media centers will help you feel comfortable in situations never discussed in your course work.

You learned how materials are cataloged, heard about automation, reference sources, databases, and the Internet, and were told to read *Information Power*. What you didn't spend much time on and will discover in this very practical guide is how to

- conduct yourself at a job interview
- get started once you are hired
- find the most important people you will need to work with
- connect with your students (beyond teaching lessons)
- get along with teachers
- have a good relationship with your principal

- run the media center (from preparing budgets to dealing with vendors)
- become an advocate and publicize your program
- determine your philosophy
- deal with subjects such as intellectual freedom, copyright, plagiarism, and your professional growth

When you step into a new position, so many things are thrown at you so fast that you end up just focusing on the immediate details. We hope this book gives you a way to view your job as a whole, starting by developing a philosophy that unifies everything you do, allowing you to make connections among its often competing elements. By keeping in mind this larger view, you will stay more on track and be less likely to feel overwhelmed. This also prevents you from operating with a "duct tape and fire extinguisher" approach in which you *react* to situations rather than being prepared for them. Just keep in mind that there is *no way* you can accomplish everything in your first year. However, while it takes at least five years to establish an exemplary program, you should feel you are heading in the right direction by the time your first school year ends.

If you are experienced and moving to a new location, it may appear in some places as if we are giving too many details, but for those of you just starting out the additional information can be reassuring, reinforcing your already good instincts. Accept the fact that you will make some mistakes. You're only human. Learn from them and move on.

It has always been a guiding principle for us to write in such a way that our readers are not put to sleep after a long working day. While superintendents, principals, and other administrators can be either male or female, we refer to superintendents as "he" and to principals as "she" throughout, rather than using the awkward "he or she." We have also used the abbreviations SLMS, SLMP, and LMC for the terms *school library media specialist* (i.e., you), *school library media program* (your program), and *library media center* (your facility), respectively.

WHAT YOU WILL FIND IN THE CHAPTERS

Beginning with a discussion of *Information Power,* chapter 1 discusses your philosophy and how it relates to everything you will be doing on the job, as well as introducing the three parts of your school community—

students, teachers, and administrators (all covered in greater depth in later chapters). From there, chapter 2, "Getting the Job," walks you through everything from your resume and application to the interview and follow-up.

Once you have accepted a position, chapter 3, "Finding Your Way," helps you view your library media center as others see it, check the collection, acquaint yourself with the building layout, meet the faculty and staff, and learn about your district and community.

Chapter 4, "Getting Yourself Organized," focuses on ferreting out information before the school year begins; highlights policies important to your job, such as the absolutely critical selection policy (telling you how to prepare one if there is none), the acceptable use policy, and other documents; discusses how to handle your schedule, whether rigid or flexible; suggests how to spruce up your space and prepare your office; advises how and from whom to order everything you need; and describes how to handle purchase orders.

The next three chapters—chapter 5, "Reaching Your Students," chapter 6, "Reaching Your Teachers," and chapter 7, "A Matter of Principals"—offer you detailed information and suggestions for the many aspects of dealing with these most important people in your working life. Chapter 6 also provides an effective plan for running an author's visit.

Chapter 8, "Advocacy and You," defines the difference between public relations, marketing, and advocacy, and describes your relationship with volunteers and parents in general, as well as school board members and business and community groups outside the school.

Chapter 9 explores various types of planning under many different circumstances: everything you need to know about your budget, buying books and periodicals, obtaining alternative funds (and even running a book fair), collection mapping, weeding, and managing your support staff.

"Technology and You," chapter 10, begins with the key issue of becoming friendly with the technology department, something that can make your job much easier. It also talks about filters and unblocking sites, acceptable use policies in action, online databases, library management systems, and what to do if your vendor goes out of business and your system is no longer supported.

Chapter 11, "Ethics, Standards, and You," incorporates professional and individual ethics into your program—including how to combat the problem of plagiarism—and explains the driving forces of national and state standards.

Chapter 12, "Looking Back, Looking Forward," brings your year to a close, but, in addition to providing details on how to manage this, mirrors chapter 1 in going beyond the basics of your job to address more weighty issues. By knowing what being a professional entails, you will return after the summer vacation ready to take your school library media program to an even higher level.

Two additional aids appear as appendixes. "Essential Resources" lists titles for your professional shelf and websites to bookmark. "Jobbers and Vendors" names some major companies that support the library market. Following the appendixes, a glossary identifies some key terms used in libraries and education.

Depending on what you need to know at the moment, read or flip through the chapters, using the index if you want a quick answer, to give you replies to questions and problems that all of us face. Look at the "Key Ideas" (important concepts to take away with you) at the end of each chapter. Use the interactive boxes after major topics to help you think through what you have just read and anticipate what you would do in similar circumstances. Even though you have been taught that it is wrong to write in a book, do not hesitate to jot your responses in these boxes—perhaps in pencil. You may change your mind as time passes and can then erase or add to your original comments.

WHAT IS NOT IN THIS BOOK

Although we have written many books about how to present information literacy skills to students and how to collaborate with teachers, none of this is included here. (You can check our website, http://www.school-librarians-workshop.com, for examples of that information.) Our focus in this book is on all the critical aspects of doing a great job that are not discussed anywhere else in the literature.

We wish you well as you begin this phase of your career, and we remember when we were once in your shoes. After Ruth received her M.L.S. degree, she realized she did not know how to select and purchase books. Colleagues came to her aid and she soon figured it out. Years later, after she and Hilda had published a number of books and had begun writing and editing *The School Librarian's Workshop,* her former professor commented that these resources were a great asset since they dealt with "all the things that hadn't been covered in library school." With *New on the Job,* we hope to be your guide through what is often an overwhelming challenge.

Good luck!

CHAPTER 1

Your Philosophy

I think, therefore I am a school library media specialist.

*T*ypically the workday for any school library media specialist (SLMS) begins as soon as the door to the library media center (LMC) is open and ends when it is closed because, unlike teachers, you can always expect that someone will drop in who is grateful to see that you are there. Your job is often frenetic and disjointed as you move from one class, teacher, student, or parent to another with no logic and, most often, without being able to complete any one task before having to move on to the next. In such an environment, it is easy to lose track of a large overall design for what you are doing.

As the quotes sprinkled throughout this chapter suggest, how you begin sets the tone for everything that will follow. You do not want to launch your new position by plunging into its myriad details without something to anchor you and provide a framework for what you are about to do. You need to determine what your philosophy is and what vision you want to hold for your school library media program (SLMP). While you have a natural urge to get down to practicalities, having a philosophy and vision in place will serve as a foundation for the many decisions and choices you will be called upon to make.

BEGIN WITH *INFORMATION POWER*

According to *Merriam-Webster's Collegiate Dictionary,* a philosophy is "a theory underlying or regarding a sphere of activity or thought." The first chapter of *Information Power: Building Partnerships for Learning* discusses the philosophical base for the standards that guide the profession.[1] While you probably know that book, now is a good time to reread those pages, become familiar with these concepts, and start out with a solid underpinning for your SLMP.

Notice that philosophy and mission are discussed in chapter 1, "The Vision." These three terms are sometimes used interchangeably, so you need to be clear about what they mean. Philosophy is rooted in beliefs; mission explains purpose; and vision is about how you wish to be perceived. Although several pages are devoted to the subject, it is important that your philosophy, your mission, and particularly your vision are fairly brief so they can be easily recalled. If you need to look them up, they are not really part of how you manage your program.

Among the *philosophical* statements in *Information Power* are the core beliefs that the SLMP "must be dynamic, enthusiastic, and student centered" and that the SLMS is "the essential link who [connects] students, teachers, and others with the information resources they need."[2] The *mission* is clearly spelled out in one sentence: "The mission of the library media program is to ensure that students and staff are effective users of ideas and information."[3] The bulleted ideas beneath this passage detail what is necessary to achieve the mission. The vision has the SLMP playing a "unique and pivotal role in the learning community" and is "based on three central ideas: collaboration, leadership, and technology."[4]

Well begun is half done.

Aristotle

Once you are comfortable with terminology and major points, check to see if there is an existing philosophy statement for your school or district and the SLMP. High schools evaluated by an accrediting agency invariably have such a statement for the school. Review any of these to see how well they are aligned with what is in *Information Power.* You want to be sure that your program emphasizes the core ideas of the national standards, but you should also recognize that the SLMP must demonstrate how it advances the school's or district's concerns.

In most cases, you should find many places of common ground between the philosophical statements. An existing SLMP's philosophy statement might not need any tweaking, and the only thing necessary is for you to implement it as you plan for the future and conduct your daily routines. If changes are required, make them for your own use until such time as you have established yourself. You can then suggest a small committee of faculty, parents, and, in middle and high schools, students to help develop a new philosophy statement.

Creating a Philosophy and Vision

What words do you want to include in your philosophy?

_____

What words do you want to include in your mission? (You might want to use the mission statement given in *Information Power.*)

_____

What words do you want to include in your vision?

_____

Use these terms to create a draft of each.

YOUR PHILOSOPHY AND THE SCHOOL COMMUNITY

Once you have a working philosophy in place, you will need to keep it in mind as you meet and get to know students, teachers, and administrators. While your philosophy will affect your dealings with others, these three groups are the ones you will be working with on a daily basis.

Students

However you worded your philosophy, you undoubtedly indicated that the SLMP needs to be student centered. What does this really mean? If you ran a business and you had just identified your most important customers, how would you treat them?

Chapter 5 of this book goes into detail about the relationship you will build with your students, but the first step is to acknowledge that they are the reason you are there. If they dislike you and hate being in the LMC, nothing you do will matter. While this statement may seem extreme, and many will not recognize its truth, the fact is that your impact on students is heavily affected by the way you interact with them.

When students withdraw from you, the cost can be high. You can teach, grade, and demonstrate that they have attained certain skills, but you will have failed to show them the role libraries can play in their lives. One of the underlying messages of every lesson you present is that learning is more than just something students do for a good grade. It leads to their growth as individuals. When they explore topics, the knowledge they gain becomes a part of who they are.

However, if students are disengaged, they will not hear the lesson, let alone your ultimate goal. If they don't hear the lesson, they are less likely to seek information for its own sake. If they don't seek information for its own sake, they will not become lifelong learners.

Teachers

While being student centered is your focus, access to students is through teachers. Even if you are in a rigidly scheduled elementary school, teachers' attitude toward you will affect how students perceive you. Connecting with teachers is an essential aspect of your philosophy and job. They need to see the program's "dynamism" and to feel that you are eager to meet their information needs.

Although chapter 6 focuses on specifics for developing, maintaining, and expanding your relationship with teachers, you need to pay attention to this from the beginning. The first step is to acknowledge that *you* are the one responsible for creating this vital link. From their perspective, teachers are doing fine without you. What do you have to offer them?

Starting on day one, you have to be proactive, seeking them out and establishing a collegial bond.

You will probably develop personal friendships with faculty members, but, unlike them, you must not actively dislike anyone. In order to implement your philosophy, demonstrate your mission, and achieve your vision, you must get along, at least on a professional level, with each teacher in the school. Every staff member is entitled to receive your best possible service.

Administrators

Principals and supervisors are usually not incorporated into your philosophy, but you will be more successful if they know and support it. You will frequently hear SLMSs bemoaning that administrators have little awareness of what they do. Large-group instruction, creating a budget, and buying books and supplies seem to be administrators' concept of the sum total of your job. As a result, they observe your teaching only as part of the formal observation process, ignoring everything else you do.

In chapter 7 you will discover ways to bridge this gap in understanding, but, as with teachers, the responsibility is yours. You must be the one to reach out to administrators and do so in ways that will get you heard and respected. Complaining is easier than finding the right approach to communicating regularly and positively with your principal, but the rewards of the latter are well worth it.

Your objective in all your dealings with administrators is to have them recognize the scope of what you do and how it increases student learning and achievement. To be successful, you must present yourself as a team player and the SLMP as part of the solution.

The Big Three

With which of these three groups (students, teachers, administrators) do you think it will be easiest to build a relationship?

_____

Which of the three groups do you think will prove the most challenging?

_____

What aspects of your philosophy will most appeal to each group?

_____

YOUR PHILOSOPHY AND YOUR JOB

In library school, being an SLMS seemed rather simple. You developed or carried out the SLMP, which entailed working with students and teachers, teaching classes, ordering print and online resources, demonstrating their use, and providing open access to ideas and information. But once you are on the job, it sometimes feels as though these critical areas take a back seat to the many other demands placed on you.

As you cope with many things that you had not expected, your philosophy will once again serve you well. No matter what you are asked to do, filter it through your core beliefs so that you can view all your tasks as advancing the SLMP's fundamental values in some way.

Scope of Your Job

The first place to determine what you are expected to do is the official job description. You might be surprised to discover what is required and what is missing. Are you expected to have a "duty period" which may take you out of the LMC? Is your day longer than that of classroom teachers?

Although some of the duties in your job description seem extraneous to your primary function, approach them from your philosophical base.

The unexamined life is not worth living.

Socrates

Instead of seeing them as tasks that detract from what you are trying to do, look for ways to use them to further your SLMP. At the elementary school level, you may be assigned bus duty. Rather than regarding it as an annoyance, embrace the opportunity to greet or say good-bye to students for the day. This is one more way of building your relationship with them. Even better, offer to keep the LMC open for the same amount of time as the required duty would take so as to increase access for students, teachers, and parents.

Do not overlook what is generally the final item listed in the job description. It usually reads something like, "and all other duties deemed appropriate." As you have probably guessed, you are not the one who determines whether a duty is appropriate. This umbrella clause can cover a lot of surprising territory, including covering for teachers (even in physical education classes) when the office cannot find substitutes.

Whatever you may think of your job description, you will not be able to change it easily. The board of education passed it, and board action is required to alter it. However, you can sometimes be creative in how you accomplish some of the tasks in the description. For example, when substituting, you can ask to meet with the class in the LMC. If the teacher did not leave a detailed plan, you might be able to adapt what you are given to include aspects of information literacy.

Other Jobs

Among the jobs you may not have anticipated are caring for aging copier machines, finding information for teachers' children, performing reference services for parents, or being called on to help with a computer or printer problem in a classroom because it is easier to ask you than to get someone from the district technology department (if the district even has one). Just because these tasks were not listed in your job description does not mean you should refuse to do them.

The worst thing you can do for your program and your own future in the school is to respond either in your tone of voice or body language with, "When did this get to be *my* job?" If one of the phrases in your philosophy statement is about being an "essential link," you can view any of those "special requests" as an opportunity to show the diversified ways you make a contribution to the school community.

In every situation, the choice as to what to do is yours. Some SLMSs look on these assorted tasks as showing a lack of respect for their professionalism. After a while, their attitude will send a message and they will get fewer people asking for this type of help. However, there is a cost. They are perceived as difficult and complaining. Taking care of these jobs will consume some of your precious time, but if you do them graciously you build friendships and earn respect as someone who can be counted on in a pinch.

In middle or high schools you might be expected to serve as an adviser for a class, club, or team. Any of these gives you access to students in a less structured setting, allowing you and the students to get to know each other better. Whether you coach them for an academic competition or meet with graphic novel fans, you will learn a lot about how they think, what they like and don't like, and what they want from the LMC. This contact is invaluable.

Tech Takeover

The balance of your job is increasingly being skewed toward technology. In the early days of "AV," this meant setting up 16-mm film projectors and changing lamps in overhead projectors. Later it necessitated managing VCRs and setting up carts for the classroom, often keeping track of them as they went in and out of the LMC. Sometimes the SLMS was the one expected to videotape class and school events.

Several of these jobs will still be part of your responsibilities, but numerous others have been added. Many SLMSs are now webmasters for their school's web page as well as the one for the LMC. Once again, turn to your philosophy to see how these added duties fit. While many of these duties help you become a more visible presence in the school, others take away more than they add to what you are trying to accomplish.

Eliminating these tasks takes time and patience. If they are not in your job description (aside from "all other duties deemed appropriate"), you might be able to make changes later. After you have built up your credibility with your principal, you can discuss how these added responsibilities are preventing you from developing the SLMP in specific ways. Be prepared with ideas as to who would be the more logical persons to get them done.

Added Teaching

Although rigidly scheduled SLMSs anticipate having classes most of the day, you may be surprised to discover that you have been assigned to teach computer classes or are expected to teach a basic skills reading class. At middle or high school, you might be required to provide a course on the research process. Since such a course is disconnected from other teachers' classroom activities, the topics you might suggest for students to explore will probably have little relationship to what they are currently studying. As a result, much less learning occurs than when you develop an assignment in collaboration with teachers. In essence, this type of course poses as much of a challenge as hosting students during the teachers' prep period at the elementary school level.

Reconcile yourself to the situation. You will be unable to change these assignments for quite a while—and perhaps never. Rather than waste energy being annoyed by an administration that has no understanding of what you could accomplish without this added burden, seek ways to turn it to your advantage.

Find methods for bringing information literacy skills to computer classes you teach. Complement basic skills texts with great books from your collection to nurture a love of reading even in students who are struggling with the reading process. For middle and high school classes, talk to subject teachers at those grade levels, and see if you can collaborate on a research project that will have them grade the content areas while you do the rest.

Tasks beyond the SLMP

Which of the responsibilities described in this section did you expect?

_____

Which one (or ones) do you think should not be part of your job?

_____

What have you learned that will help you take on these tasks with a positive attitude?

_____

CAN ANYONE DO IT ALL?

You might have noticed that the extensive list of what you will be expected to do overlooked some major requirements. Your library teaching duties and the ongoing backroom tasks were among the omitted items. By now, you are probably wondering how you can possibly get everything done. It would seem to be a job for Super Librarian, for only someone with super powers would be able to accomplish it all.

A Bit of Balance

A little perspective is helpful here. First, reassure yourself. You will not be doing everything every day. While even those with a flexible schedule will almost always meet with classes, and duty periods must be attended to, you will begin to see there are spaces within your day that lend themselves to different tasks.

On the other hand, there will be times when you feel pulled in many directions simultaneously. A clear understanding of your priorities—and philosophy—is necessary so that you stay focused. Student and teacher needs always come first. That said, when you have a request (or demand) from an administrator, you must find a way to attend to it, no matter what. Accept the fact that your days are likely to be hectic, with some more so than others. Laughing at the insanity helps.

Be prepared on those difficult days to put off doing anything that does not require your immediate attention and deal with what does. Take a deep breath every now and then and remind yourself of your philosophy. It will ground you and prevent you from succumbing to feeling overwhelmed. Even more important, by keeping the sensation of being beleaguered at bay, you will not become irritable and brusque with students and teachers. Once again, laughing will get you through it.

Reality Check

One of the many aspects of your job not covered in library school is the length of your day. A few of you may even have thought that being an SLMS would be easier than being a classroom teacher because you would not have lesson plans or papers to grade. Obviously, rigidly scheduled SLMSs have both, although their lesson plans can be reused with classes at the same grade level, lessening prep time somewhat. However, that just begins to address the issue.

While flexibly scheduled SLMSs at any level are now expected to turn in lesson plans, and middle and high school SLMSs often participate in grading papers by evaluating the resources used, the non-classroom responsibilities are what really add to the length of your day. You have to make time to read professional literature, prepare purchase orders, catalog material, explore electronic databases, and weed the collection, along with a host of other tasks.

Teachers do much of their non-instructional jobs during their prep period or at home. Your duty-free time (if it is on your schedule) is likely to be taken up by staff or parents who drop in and are so happy to catch you "not doing anything." While you can read journals and do a few other tasks elsewhere, many of your jobs need to be done in the LMC.

You must face the fact that your day will extend beyond the hours in your contract. Expect to arrive early or leave late on many days—more so in your first years on the job. Most of you will not be paid for summer work, but if you don't make time to go in, you will be inundated with mail and boxes of books and supplies when school starts.

A cautionary note is necessary. You can easily get so caught up in trying to get everything done that the LMC takes over your life. Set deadlines for how late you will stay and how many days you will do so—and abide by them. Family, friends, and outside interests are vital. You will be a better SLMS if your job is not your life.

Getting Help

For your survival, accept that you cannot do it alone. If you have a support staff, learn to use it well. Few of you will have more than one clerk, but maximize this resource. Most clerks will enjoy opportunities to do more than routine tasks. Teach them to become active paraprofessionals.

If you are without support staff, find volunteers and get them excited about the contribution they are making. At middle and high schools you can create a library council. Fourth and fifth graders can also become helpers. Be sure to give them interesting tasks in addition to the mundane book shelving. For example, they can be trained to pull books for a class.

At the elementary school level, parents and senior citizens are generally your best resource. Ask for advice from the other SLMSs in the district as to how best to recruit them. While training volunteers takes time, if you engage their interest by using their talents in the LMC, they will return regularly so you can count on them. You may even discover that you have recruited new members to the profession, since your best helpers often become so enthusiastic about working in the LMC that they will go back to school for courses.

You might find yourself responsible for multiple schools and a complex schedule. Sometimes it will seem as though whatever you want is in one of the other buildings. Chapter 4 offers some helpful ideas for coping with this challenge.

Remember that you are responsible for the behavior of your support staff, whether student or adult. Their attitude toward students and teachers will affect the climate of the LMC. In part, how you treat them will carry over to how they interact with others, but you need to go further.

Talk about your philosophy, and let volunteers and support staff see how it informs your actions. Encourage them to ask about your decisions, so they can see how you are guided by your philosophy in specific situations. Through these discussions they see how your philosophy comes into play on a daily basis, and in assimilating it they too will incorporate the concepts as the natural way of dealing with any and all of your users.

A journey of a thousand miles must begin with a single step.

Lao-tzu

A Full Plate

Which tasks do you think have medium priority? (This may change as you become more familiar with your job.)

_____

Which do you think have the lowest priority?

_____

How many days a week will you extend your hours?

_____

What help is already available? Where do you think you can get more?

_____

DEFINE WHO YOU ARE

Your roles and self-perception are implied although not specifically mentioned in your philosophy. Both need to be recognized and understood. *Information Power* spells out the former, but you must determine the latter.

Roles

According to *Information Power,* you are a teacher, an instructional partner, an information specialist, and a program administrator.[5] These responsibilities should be carried out in a way that attests to your philosophy. Therefore, everything you do must in some way connect to being student centered and whatever else you have incorporated into your statement.

Remind yourself that the philosophical base of your roles creates a consistency that weaves the SLMP into a unified whole. Whether you are creating a lesson plan, working at some level with a teacher, explaining how to evaluate the credibility of a website, or reviewing LMC policies, everything should always connect back to your core beliefs.

While you cannot do so on a daily basis, take time at week's end to reflect on what you have done. Did your actions and decisions put student needs at the forefront? In what ways have you enhanced others' view of the dynamism of the SLMP? How well did you link students and staff to the resources they needed?

Some weeks you will do better than others. The personal evaluation should not make you think you are failing but rather help you see where you have been most successful and which areas need more work. Think of ways you might have handled a given situation better. If you are stuck, talk with another SLMS in your district, or better yet, turn to a colleague at your school. Some state school library media associations have mentor programs or help desks. If neither is available, seek out someone whom you perceive as a leader and ask for help. You might be surprised to see how willing the person is to offer you guidance.

Self-Perception

You will often hear rigidly scheduled elementary SLMSs complain that they are babysitters, enabling teachers to get their prep time. While a rigid schedule is not the preferred approach for teaching information literacy skills or any of the other aspects of the SLMP, perceiving yourself as a babysitter just makes a bad situation worse. How can you be student centered if you feel you are just a babysitter marking time? Change that mental image and you will be amazed by the effect.

If you believe teachers are too lazy or too busy to work with you, you are likely to have your view confirmed. Unwittingly, you convey that message in your tone of voice and with your body language. Expecting that teachers will be excited by what you have to offer will very often bring positive results.

Another aspect of self-perception is how you see yourself within the school. Do you consider yourself to be a teacher or a member of the staff? An SLMS in a conversation said, "You teachers . . ." and, without recognizing it, immediately separated herself from the faculty. Be aware of pronouns. Use "we" as much as you can when discussing situations with teachers.

Time to Reflect

Which role—teacher, instructional partner, information specialist, program administrator—most easily fits your philosophy?

_____

Which role requires more effort to incorporate?

_____

What is a better view than "babysitter" for how you approach rigidly scheduled classes?

_____

WHO AM I?

What you call yourself and what others call you are not among the most significant contributors to your success, but how you handle your job title is an indicator of your self-perception and complements the image you want to create of the SLMP.

Your Title

An old nursery rhyme goes:

> *Elizabeth, Elspeth, Betsy and Bess,*
> *They all went together to seek a bird's nest;*
> *They found a bird's nest with five eggs in,*
> *They all took one, and left four in.*

The riddle is solved when you realize that Elspeth, Betsy, and Bess are variations of Elizabeth. Many years ago your title would simply have been librarian or school librarian. Today you might be called a school library media specialist, library media specialist, teacher-librarian, or a number of other variants.

This issue surfaces regularly among SLMSs. Some prefer to be called librarian. This is the term most frequently used when talking informally within the profession, primarily because it is the shortest. The main reason for using one of the alternatives is that people, recalling their school experiences, think they know what a "librarian" does. Hearing the other titles makes them aware that there is something more going on.

The American Association of School Librarians (AASL) has the older term as part of its name but now favors the title *school library media specialist*. States and school districts have selected other titles. Many prefer the term *teacher-librarian* because it reinforces the importance of the instructional role. Others see that as too limiting. The debate continues, but, if your title is not already set for you, decide what your preference is and use it consistently.

What Others Call You

No matter how frequently you employ your title, you will be referred to in many different ways. Invariably the word *librarian* will be included somehow. A principal may introduce you as the "library teacher," differentiating you in this way from the reading or computer teacher. Parents tend to address you simply as the "librarian." Teachers, wanting to be sure their students get it right, are most likely to use the title *school library media specialist* or whatever you have chosen.

Some of you are very aware that you are far more than what is implied by the term *librarian* and will explain the distinction whenever the opportunity arises. Most of you overlook the variations, considering them too unimportant within the larger context. The best approach is someplace in the middle, although distinctly more in the category of "do not overreact."

Never correct anyone for what they call you. As noted, the nomenclature is confusing enough within the profession. On the other hand, find subtle ways of reinforcing your proper title. When you speak with that person on another occasion, you can mention your proper title within the conversation. At another time, you can discuss the variety of names for SLMSs and explain why you are no longer called a "librarian."

Why should it matter, and do you really need to bother? Again, this is not a major issue. The question, as always, is how does your title reflect your philosophy? By reminding people of *why* you are called an SLMS (or whatever else is used), you are also sharing what you believe in a subtle way.

Key Ideas

■ The terms *philosophy, mission,* and *vision* are sometimes used interchangeably, but they are different, and you need all three.

■ Your philosophy will form the basis for your dealings with the educational community and the way you structure the SLMP.

■ You are the one responsible for creating relationships with students, teachers, and administrators.

■ You will be required to do some jobs that seem remote from the responsibilities of an SLMS.

■ Using some creativity, you can align these added tasks with your philosophy.

■ Remembering your priorities will keep you focused during the busiest days.

■ Look for the fun in the wonderful insanity of an incredibly hectic day.

■ Your days will extend beyond contract hours.

■ Share your philosophy with your volunteers and support staff.

■ Know your roles and yourself in order to present what you do in the best possible way.

■ Be consistent in what you call yourself.

■ Your philosophy and *Information Power* are a behind-the-scenes presence every day.

NOTES

1. American Association of School Librarians, Association for Educational Communications and Technology, *Information Power: Building Partnerships for Learning* (Chicago: American Library Association, 1998), 1–7.
2. Ibid., 2.
3. Ibid., 6.
4. Ibid., 4.
5. Ibid., 4–5.

It is best to begin at the beginning.

Glinda in *The Wizard of Oz*

CHAPTER 2

Getting the Job

I am going to soar like an eagle!

Resume

A shortage of school library media specialists does not mean that you can be casual about job hunting. The right job, the perfect situation for you will always require that you be at your best from start to finish.

YOUR RESUME

The first step in any job search is to be sure that your resume is current *and* focused on the position you want. For many of you, school librarianship is a second career. It is tempting to prove that you have been successful in the past by listing all the employers you have had and the titles you have held. While the interviewers will be interested in knowing this, if you want them to pay attention, address how these experiences will be beneficial to you as an SLMS.

For example, if you have had a career in sales, instead of noting that you increased floor traffic, point to your facility in creating eye-catching displays that lure people in (you will be doing the same in the library media center). Rather than talk about increases in customers and sales, identify your relationship skills. Highlight your knowledge of technology and your expertise in organization and communication.

Include a section titled "Related Experiences" in your resume. Here you can list your field experience, volunteer work with youth groups, substitute teaching, and so on. If you have not done any of this as yet, definitely get on the substitute list at several school districts in your area. If you do well, the teachers who like your work can be references.

Avoid the now-clichéd "Objective" section. Obviously you want a "challenging opportunity to develop or expand a school library media program." This statement is boring and tells interviewers nothing. Instead, provide a list of your best qualities and abilities in a "Profile" section at the top. Keep it brief—no more than three or four sentences. If you use bullets, three are the minimum and five the maximum. The information you give under "Experience" should show evidence of what you highlighted in the "Profile."

List the relevant associations to which you belong. If you are serious about your career, you should already be a member of your state association for SLMSs, and it is an excellent idea to belong to a national association as well. The AASL is the largest and best known of these. (Since it is a division of the American Library Association [ALA], you must join it as well.) Others to consider include the Association for Educational Communications and Technology and the International

Society for Technology in Education. Although membership dues can be expensive, most organizations have reduced rates for students. Consider it part of the cost of doing your job, no different from having a career wardrobe or keeping gas in your car.

New SLMSs, and even old hands, generally fail to include a "Professional Activities" section on their resume. If you have served on a committee for any of the aforementioned organizations or been a presenter at a workshop at one of their conferences, this is the place to list these. Even if you have not had these experiences, note any conferences or institutes you have attended. You will be demonstrating your commitment to expanding your knowledge and expertise, the hallmarks of a true professional.

References are checked, so be sure to choose them wisely. Avoid having only professors. You want people who can speak about your different strengths. When you ask someone to be a reference, continue the conversation to ascertain whether they have any reservations about you. Do not argue with them if they do; just don't list them. It is better to know in advance who will be giving you a wholehearted endorsement.

If at all possible, find a library supervisor or someone else who hires SLMSs and ask them to look over your resume. Have them tell you what they think of it. Is there something that should not be in the resume? Have you missed anything important? Does it look good? Should it be formatted differently?

Finally, proofread your resume. Spell-check notwithstanding, it is amazing how many finished resumes contain spelling and grammatical errors. Along with your cover letter, the resume is the first impression that interviewers receive of you. You do not want to appear to be slipshod—or worse.

Resumes and Job Hunting

Which aspects of your previous work experiences can make you a more effective SLMS?

_____

Check the website for your state library association. What information does it have that is helpful for you?

_____

Identify three people who can provide references for different facets of your abilities.

_____

COVER LETTERS

What impression do you want to give interviewers? Cover letters say much more than the few lines they contain. While you don't want to be long-winded, one paragraph is far too brief. Most letters have three short paragraphs, but they tend to be very dry and boring. Flippancy does not work, and neither does loading the letter with jargon to impress administrators with your erudition. However, you do need to promote yourself.

There is little you can do to change what goes in the opening sentence. You simply state how you came to apply for the position, such as "In response to the advertisement appearing in the *Chronicle* on May 12, I am enclosing my resume for your attention." The question is, where do you go from there?

A good follow-up—and one that is rarely used—is to briefly explain why the position interests you. Research the school district so you can refer to characteristics about it that appeal to you. Perhaps you want the challenge of making a difference in an urban environment. Or you might want an opportunity to work with the best and the brightest in some upper socioeconomic location. There is always a good reason for wanting to be in a particular school system. Once you know what the one you are applying to is like, you can champion its uniqueness in your letter.

The middle paragraph is where you really sell yourself. Be careful not to use terms such as *information literacy skills* that are not always familiar to those outside the profession. You can bring them up during the interview, where you can explain them as you go along.

Keep the focus on why you are an excellent candidate for the job. Do not restate your resume. Highlight your special abilities; for example, "I know that the combination of my course work and extensive background in sales and marketing will help me raise everyone's awareness of how the library media program [*do not use acronyms in your letter*] can improve student achievement." Add one or two more ideas, such as "I hope to work with teachers as an equal partner to incorporate technology and 21st-century skills into the curriculum."

What you are doing with these sentences is setting up what will happen in the interview. You will be questioned as to how you plan to do the things you mention. Knowing these are coming, you will be more prepared to respond confidently.

The traditional closing is "I look forward to hearing from you." Expand on it slightly and say something like, "I look forward to discussing with you what I can contribute to the school program." Indicate whether you would like to be reached via phone or e-mail and provide numbers and addresses.

The waiting now begins, and it can be wearing. If you hear nothing for a week, call the human relations department (or the person to whom you sent your information). Verify that your application letter was received and ask when interviews will be scheduled. You may be told that no date has been set as yet. In that case, call back no less than two weeks later. Do not complain about the slow pace and be gracious on the telephone.

Cover Letters with Clout

What type of situation do you really want?

_____

What one sentence can show why you will be an ideal fit for the position?

_____

What questions do you think you will be asked based on your cover letter?

_____

THE INTERVIEW

Finally, you receive a call to schedule an interview. In the elation of the moment, you probably just set up a convenient time and date, but much work needs to be done before the day arrives. If you did not think to do so when you were asked to come in, telephone the secretary with whom you spoke and find out who will be present. Your preparation will be slightly different if the principal is conducting the interview alone, as opposed to the SLMS or a department chair also being part of the process.

Getting Ready

Be sure you know how to get to the location. A dry run is always a good idea. You don't want to be trying to read directions when you are nervous. Be sure to build in extra time to get there. Arriving too early is far better than being late. You still might make a wrong turn, or traffic can be worse than anticipated. Allow time to find a parking space and the entrance. In numerous places this is a problem. High schools in particular often have limited room for visitors, and at all levels security concerns have led to many doors being locked once the day begins.

Dress appropriately. While a suit will always show a man at his best, a tie and sport jacket are generally sufficient for most school districts. Women should avoid overly high heels, short skirts, or outfits that are too tight or low-cut. You may be given a tour of the building and should be able to keep pace with the interviewer without difficulty.

Prepare a portfolio of your best lessons and projects. If this is your first job as an SLMS, you can use something you did while interning, or even samples of your class work. In addition to hard copy, have a CD ready to leave with the interviewers. Whether or not it is looked at is less important than your demonstrating that you have teaching skills (although if you are asked back, you will probably have to present a lesson) and are tech savvy.

Carry your portfolio in something attractive. A colored plastic envelope which you can get at the mega-stationery stores will work well. Clip your business card to the paper copy, because you will want to leave this with the interviewer.

Interview Essentials

What will your interview outfit be?

_____

What are you going to include in your portfolio?

_____

Managing the Meeting

You are now appropriately dressed and on time. You have your portfolio with you, and the interviewer greets you and ushers you into an office or conference room. Have a plan of action in mind so that you are focused rather than letting your nerves get the best of you.

Say the names of the people as you are introduced so that you can remember them. If you forget one, do not try to fake it. Ask to have it repeated.

Unless you are directed to a specific seat, choose your chair with some care. You want to be able to see everyone without having to twist around. This will enable you to view other people's reactions to questions and answers without making it obvious that you are observing them. If necessary, move your chair before you sit down. Obviously, this is not a concern if only one person is conducting the interview.

Place your briefcase or portfolio next to your seat. Be sure any material that you want for the interview is easy to remove. Handbags should be out of the way so they are not a distraction. Sit decorously. Particularly if you are in an office, you should be mindful of your legs. Women keep them crossed at the ankle. Men can put their leg across their knee but must be careful not to take up too much space or slouch in an overly relaxed posture. You should appear attentive.

After a general greeting, the interview will get under way. Your cover letter and resume are usually the basis for the opening questions. Even though you are expecting these, take time to phrase your answers. Seek a balance between being overly brief and going on at length. If you use any library jargon, such as "information literacy" or "effective and efficient users of information and ideas," be sure to define them. You might say something like, "Research projects should incorporate information literacy skills which include such concepts as evaluating the accuracy of Internet websites and understanding how to avoid plagiarism." Never assume that administrators know library terminology.

Look for an opportune moment to introduce your portfolio. Explain what it contains and let the interviewers know that you are leaving it with them so they can review it when they have the time. Suggest that if they have any questions about it, you will be happy to answer them.

As the interview progresses, you are likely to be asked to respond to hypothetical scenarios or to envision the LMC of the future. Pause before answering. Think of two or three key points you want to make. Highlight them as you present your answer. You can use this time to inform administrators about important aspects of the SLMP as long as you do not appear to be lecturing them.

To prepare for this phase, ask any friends who are SLMSs or even fellow students to come up with "scenario" questions. See how well you think on your feet as you answer these questions. Even if you find it difficult, after a few examples you will have some important ideas that can be incorporated into your responses during the real thing.

Interview Prep

Visualize the opening of your interview. What are you carrying? Did you keep your right hand free so that you could extend it for the greeting?

_____

You are asked, "What do you think are the biggest challenges in preparing students for the world they will face?" How will you answer?

_____

How would you respond to this scenario? Three teachers ask you for classroom collections on the same subject for the same time. How will you handle it?

_____

Questions to Ask

Most candidates for school positions come to interviews expecting to be asked questions and hoping they will come up with good answers. Such a passive attitude does not suggest that you will be a proactive SLMS. Worse, at some point the principal or whoever is conducting the meeting will say, "Do you have any questions for me (us)?" If you are not prepared, you will either mumble something to the effect that you have nothing to ask at this time or will make the ultimate gaffe and want to know what the salary will be.

Prepare in advance. Look upon the interview process as a giant reference question. Research the district and school more thoroughly than you did for your cover letter. At the very least you should know the size of the student body. Try to find out how many SLMSs the district has and whether you will have any support staff.

Check to see if the school or the LMC has a web page, and explore it to collect further information. What does the school brag about? Is the mission statement on the page? If it is not too formulaic, you will gain some understanding of the environment.

Your findings will suggest a number of questions you can ask at the interview. At a middle or high school, you might want to ask how many classes use the LMC in the course of a month or year and which departments schedule most heavily. Are there any special activities or projects that rely on the services of the SLMP? For an elementary school, you want to be clear about whether there is a rigid or a flexible schedule. Unfortunately, most are rigid, with the SLMS taking teachers' classes during their preparation time. In that case, you want to discover whether you have any open time blocks which can be used for collaborative projects. If nothing else, asking this question raises administrators' awareness of the advantages of a flexible schedule.

Asking what the hours are or if you have any duty assignments has a negative connotation. You can request to see the SLMS's schedule, and that will give you some idea of what a typical day or week is like. Have the interviewer explain any "open" blocks, if necessary.

Find out why the position is available. Is it a new one? If not, why is the current SLMS leaving? Will it be possible for you to have a conversation with that person? Be alert for evasive answers which would indicate that the departure was not a pleasant one.

It is equally important to discuss the technology setup in the LMC. Is it automated? Does the interviewer know what system is used? Ask to see the facility. Depending on how much time you are given, you will be able to make some assessments as to how current things are. You can do a quick count of the computers and then check to find out what version of the operating system they are running and when new hardware was last purchased.

Sometimes there is a second interview with a demonstration of your teaching ability. Should that be required, be sure you are clear not only as to the content, but also the grade and ability level of the students you will be instructing. Find out how much time you will have. Ask if there is a preferred lesson plan form you should use. Try to visit the LMC to identify the resources available to students. This also gives you an opportunity to get additional information from the SLMS. If this is your first SLMS job, ask one of your professors or an experienced colleague to look over your lesson. A second set of eyes is always helpful.

Time to Reflect

What three questions would you ask an interviewer?

_____

_____

_____

Expectations—Theirs and Yours

During the interview, you must discover what the administrators and the school district really expect of you and the SLMP. It may sound as though you are all talking about the same thing, but the words can have different meanings. What does an active SLMP mean? You are envisioning exciting collaborations with teachers and students engaged in their learning. They are thinking of every seat filled and students borrowing two books whenever their class comes to the LMC.

Create a basis for understanding by finding out what administrators think are the best aspects of the current program. What changes—if any—do they want? Do they have any goals they would like you to meet by the end of your first year?

Listen carefully to their answers. Do not accept generalities such as "We want the LMC to be the heart of the school." Administrators say this and have no idea what it means. For some, this suggests the ideal location for social events. While remaining most concerned with how you are presenting yourself, be attuned to other messages you are getting. Your interviewer will also be selling the school to you. In the course of this, you will get an idea of what the principal's vision is or what she most wants to achieve. This knowledge will be very helpful to you if you get the job.

Once you are more aware of what the administration's requirements are, be sure your own expectations are likely to be met. Discuss the district's policy on professional days. Mention which conferences you want to attend and *why*. See if the interviewer is warmly supportive of this or is trying to slide past it.

Are there any other items that you assume will be part of your job? Whether it is about keeping the LMC open after school (with or without pay), summer work, or whatever is on your mind, ask about it now. Once you are hired, it is too late to say that you did not know something or were not told about it. If you are at a high school, be sure to find out whether study halls are held in the LMC. Although not widespread, this practice exists in enough places that you need to check on it. Having blocks of time filled with students who have no work (or claim to have none) and no desire to be there not only saps your time and attention, but interferes with scheduling classes for research projects.

Examining Expectations

What do you think are some expectations the school district will have?

_____

What are your expectations?

_____

What questions can you ask to see if your assumptions are accurate?

_____

Reality Check

Job hunting is a lot like applying for college. You approach it with the attitude of "please, please, pick me." But saying yes to either an employer or a college should not be based solely on the fact that they asked you. You need to consider whether or not it will be a good fit for you.

An SLMS who ran her own high school LMC was delighted to get an offer from another school district which had two professionals. The job would pay significantly more money, and the second SLMS was her friend. Within a year, the friendship had dissolved. After two years, she transferred to a middle school. The SLMS in this story was accustomed to doing things her way. Her friend had a different operating style, and, being the senior person, was the one in charge. Money will not make you happy in a position that is wrong for you.

Another SLMS considered changing to another district, but she would also be changing her level, moving from high school to elementary school. She realized that there was a rigid schedule which was counter to the way she wanted to run the LMC, but thought she might be able to modify the situation. Believing she was being reasonable, she asked the principal if he were open to a pilot program with one or two teachers to see how a flexible schedule would work. He was quite clear that he had no interest in trying it. She turned down the job.

Before you accept a job offer, review your interview. Did any red flags come up? Are the requirements and the situation consistent with your philosophy? Unless you are absolutely desperate, do not take a position where you disagree with practices before you start.

Deciding on a Job Offer

What would cause you to turn down a job offer?

_____

Are there any circumstances in which you would consider a position that had aspects contrary to your philosophy? If so, how would you plan to manage it?

_____

What is a gracious way to refuse a job?

_____

AFTER THE INTERVIEW

The period after the interview may be the most difficult time of the process. You are stuck waiting, reviewing everything you said or did not say, and wondering whether or not they liked you. Try not to obsess too much. The good news is that in one to four weeks you should have your answer.

Following Up

You might have heard that it is a good idea to send a thank-you note after the interview. That is true, but if all you say is, "Thank you for taking the time to interview me. I am sure that I can make a great contribution to the school and district," you are wasting your time and a stamp.

Make the thank-you note count. Refer to specifics—something that was said or that you saw which impressed you. Comment on an idea that the interviewer expressed. In other words, remind them of who you are. Administrators speak with a number of people when filling positions—particularly when they have several different openings. You need to have them recall what occurred in *your* interview.

If you were given some indication of when the decision was to be made, wait a few days past that before calling. Without that information, hold off for about three weeks. Not hearing anything does not mean they are not considering you. Administrators often get so busy with other matters that they put this aside. When you do call, ask the secretary if the job has been filled as yet or when they expect to decide. Do not allow your frustration to show. Be gracious and apologize for taking up her time.

Using the Post-interview Time

Try some possible sentences for a thank-you note.

_____

Prepare how you will ask the secretary for information.

_____

Hit the Ground Running

With any luck your preparation has paid off and you get the call that the position is yours. You will be asked to come in and complete paperwork. Use this time well. Even as you choose health providers and complete tax forms, get to know the people in the office. Learn their names and ask how long they have worked for the district. While you do not want to appear to be prying, you do want to present yourself as someone who is interested in others and is looking forward to beginning the new job.

Find out where other central administration offices are located in the school. You particularly need to know where accounts payable is, since that is the office that handles purchase orders. If you are comfortable doing so, introduce yourself to the people who work there. You will probably have conversations with them during the school year. They and you will appreciate being able to put faces to voices on the telephone.

If you have not had a chance to see the LMC in action as yet, try to set up a time when you can visit. Observe the number of students and teachers present and the level of activity. Note how individual students are handled when they come in. Get a sense of whether students and faculty feel comfortable and enjoy being there. If there is a support staff—or volunteers—do they seem part of the larger whole, or are they relegated to their assigned tasks somewhere distant from the action?

Talk with the SLMS to get a sense of what the priorities have been. What has been working? Are there any areas that cause problems? What information is available to help you as you take on your new duties?

In speaking with teachers, students, and LMC personnel on this visit, keep your opinions to yourself. While you cannot help making judgments, you should not share them with others. For one thing, you may not be right. You can misinterpret what you are seeing. Moreover, you do not want people who are just getting to know you to sense that you disapprove of some things they are doing.

You can help students if you notice they are struggling. (You may want to check with the teacher or the SLMS to find out if it is all right for you to do this, but generally no one has any objections.) You will get a great sense of satisfaction in being able to interact with them, knowing that they will soon be your responsibility. It also enables you to make those first tentative relationship-building steps.

Find out if there is any problem with your coming in during the summer break. You will save yourself a lot of headaches and feel more ready for opening day if you have a chance to sort through mail and organize the incoming books and supplies. Having a clerk makes the task much easier, but even if you have someone who works full-time in the summer, you will feel more comfortable if you have taken this opportunity to become familiar with some of the clerical aspects of your job.

Paying a Visit

What would you look for on your first visit to the LMC?

_____

What non-confrontational questions would you ask the SLMS?

_____

HONEYMOON PHASE

Once you are settled in your new job, you might be able to take advantage of your "honeymoon." After reading chapter 3, you will probably have an idea of some changes you would like to make. Even if the principal has only paid lip service to the idea of the SLMP being a vital part of the school community, you have an access point for discussion with her.

For example, if the collection in general—or a single area such as reference—is in dire need of updating, now is the time to call attention to the problem. What you would be looking for in this case is either an increase in the dollar figure allotted for print resources or a one-time infusion of money directed to fill a specific need. Depending on how closely the district handles finances, money may or may not be available for this school year. However, now is the time when next year's budget is being planned, so you should get your request in early—when it is likely to be granted.

Another possible area to bring to your principal's attention is the need for more assistance. You will not get them to hire someone, but at middle and high schools you might be able to have teachers assigned to the LMC as their duty period. At schools of all levels you can ask to have school substitutes, who may have extra time because of miscommunications, sent to you. By the time this is in place, you can prepare some ongoing projects for them to work on.

Whatever you ask for, be sure you never seem to be looking for ways to minimize your workload. Everything should be connected to how it will improve student achievement. Not only is this the best way to get attention, but it also reinforces the value of the SLMP.

Finally, learn early the best way to communicate with your principal or supervisor. Some prefer e-mail and respond quickly to those messages. Others like to speak with you in person. Find out whether they wish to do this before or after school or if they can be reached during the day. With a few, you must write memos. If that is the only available approach you will have to use it, but follow them up with a quick call or pop your head in the office to say you have sent something.

Communication Basics

Consider the two possible requests discussed (i.e., increased funding and increased assistance). How would you connect these to student achievement?

_____

How would you learn your principal's or supervisor's preferred communication mode?

_____

Key Ideas

- Show how your previous work experiences will make you a better SLMS.
- Avoid starting your resume with an "Objective" section.
- Belong to library and educational associations and put them on your resume.
- Select references with care.
- Review your resume before sending it off.
- Tweak the traditional format of the cover letter so yours is a bit different without being unconventional.
- Plan carefully for your interview.
- Bring a portfolio that shows you at your best.
- Research the school and district.
- Prepare perceptive questions to ask the interviewers.
- Being offered a job should not mean your automatic acceptance of it.
- Use your thank-you note to remind the interviewer of who you are.
- Arrange a visit to the LMC.
- Plan on coming in during the summer.
- Take advantage of the "honeymoon phase" to improve the SLMP.
- Learn the best way to communicate with your administrator.

CHAPTER 3

Finding Your Way

I have
an excellent
sense of direction—
will that help?

*N*ow that the job is yours, you must get oriented as rapidly as possible. Unlike teachers who have colleagues and supervisors who are ready with advice and help, you are usually alone. Your principal assumes you know what to do, and she has no idea what you require. One administrator who was wonderfully effective at leading the faculty in opening a new school told the school library media specialist who asked about supplies that there was no money or *need* for any, since all the books were ordered "fully processed." The SLMS calmly explained that even though the books were received this way, it only meant that basic cataloging information and covers were included. A property stamp, spine labels (since nothing indicated the reference or any other special collection), file folders, pads, clips, and other basics necessary for organizing an office and integrating these new resources into the collection and into the library catalog, whether it be paper or electronic, would still be necessary. The SLMS was granted a fifty-dollar "emergency" budget! She also realized that despite the principal's support, she would have to devote time and energy to educating the principal on what it takes to create an active program.

From the first you must appear confident in being able to run the SLMP. This does not mean that you cannot ask questions. Once you take stock of the situation, you will probably have plenty of them, but they will be very specific. After prioritizing these questions, you can contact the appropriate people (who they are will quite possibly be another question) to get the information you need.

YOUR NEW LIBRARY MEDIA CENTER

You have only one opportunity to make a first impression. This adage served you well when you were looking for a position, so now turn it around. You have only one chance to get a first impression of the LMC. Once you have been in a place for some time, you cease to see things that perceptive guests do. By viewing the LMC with fresh eyes, you will be able to identify changes that should be made—even if you don't get to them at once.

What Message Is It Sending?

Sometimes you meet someone and you know you are going to like them almost before they speak. At other times you have the opposite sense. We communicate in many ways other than words. The LMC does the same. Prepare yourself to observe carefully as you walk into it for the very first time. Whether or not anyone is present, does it feel welcoming? Is it a place for adults or one for students?

Try to figure out what is giving you these clues. Look around. Your instincts are responding to a number of nonverbal messages. Are posters hung on the walls? Do they look as though they have been there forever? Are rules more prominently displayed than other information? Reflect on what the room might be saying to students.

Let your eyes wander around. Is the bulletin board interesting? Does the place seem frozen twenty or so years in the past? Is it colorful or do earth tones scream 1970s at you?

If the LMC is open during your initial visit, check to see the visibility of the staff. Are they "user-friendly"? Does anyone smile at you or acknowledge your presence? How are students greeted? Look at the signage—if there is any. How visible and helpful is it?

Which shelves catch your eye first? Can you see the reference area? Are you looking at the beginning of the collection, where the bindings on multivolume encyclopedias can be very inviting? Or is the view toward the end of the section with the straggly ends of the 980s and 990s facing you? Look to see if the tops of high bookcases are being used for storage, which tends to make the room look cluttered. At the same time, unless an inventory was just done, the LMC should not be overly neat. That suggests no one is using it.

What indications do you have that this is a "media center" and not just a library? Count the computers. Are there enough for at least half a class? Is there a video display projector evident? Observe how the students and teachers use these resources. You want to see evidence that they are accessing online databases and not just doing Google searches.

Check the placement of tables and chairs as well as the height and location of book stacks. Stand at various places and note how easily you can observe students. Furniture can help or hinder discipline. If you have good sight lines, students tend to behave better, and you use less time reminding them of the proper way to act.

Finally, consider the LMC from the students' viewpoint. Is this a place where they would want to spend time, or one that they cannot wait to leave? As soon as you have some time by yourself, jot down your impressions for future reference.

First Impressions

Before checking out your new LMC, go to a public library and assess its message.
What did you notice?

_____

What are some ways to create a welcoming environment?

_____

YOUR INITIAL ASSESSMENT OF THE COLLECTION

Once you have an overall sense of the tone of the facility, you need to get an overview of the collection. Although you will assess the collection more closely later on, get a sense of it as part of your impression of the LMC as a whole. Make a quick scan of the book stacks. See if shelves are overfilled. Optimally, one fourth to one third of their space should be empty. When books are packed tightly it is hard to remove one, discouraging browsers. Worse, it is difficult to put them back. Not only does this cause students to avoid replacing titles in their proper location, but it also contributes to your workload. When adding new acquisitions or even reshelving returned items, you must spend time shifting everything in order to find a space.

Identify special sections of the collection. In addition to the obvious fiction, nonfiction, and reference sections, look for other special areas. Where are biographies (and the challenging collective biographies) kept? Are there racks for paperbacks? How many magazines are there? What does the media collection look like? Elementary schools typically keep picture books away from more difficult-to-read titles; high schools frequently have a special place for college information.

Some SLMSs prefer that the entire collection be integrated. Years ago, there was a debate on whether to shelve what was then called "AV" together with the books so that everything on a topic would be in one location. Today the recommendation is for graphic novels to be kept separate from books, and if you follow a bookstore model, you will have many different areas with which to respond to the varied interests and needs of students. Wait until you are familiar with how your students and teachers like to use the LMC before making your decision.

Do book covers look old and tired? Are many without dust jackets? The adage about not judging a book by its cover may be true, but most of us are drawn to the ones that look appealing. If too many titles seem to have been around far too long, students will not take the time to find the attractive ones buried among their aging neighbors.

Your impression of the collection is a guide to how rapidly you need to consider a weeding project. While it is best to wait a year before undertaking this task, if the situation is dire, you will have to do something. No matter how bad it is, limit yourself to weeding the most important areas—reference, science, and possibly countries and cultures. A more detailed description of how to go about weeding the collection is presented in chapter 9.

Don't overlook the electronic collection. Take time to explore what is on the computer network. See if the number and diversity of the online databases seem appropriate for the school. Revisit your initial impression over the first few months to determine what changes, if any, you wish to make. The budget for the next school year will be due before you know it, so you need to make this assessment.

To conclude your first visit, take one more tour of the facility. This will be your home. You will get to do some redecorating, but for the most part you will have to live with the larger elements—furniture, carpeting, and so on—for some time. Consider the message the LMC conveys once again. How does it reflect your philosophy? Are there any elements that conflict with your philosophy? If so, what changes can be easily made so that you will be comfortable? For you to be at your best, you have to feel content with your environment. Trust your instincts on this, and make the necessary adjustments.

Collection Considerations

Practice tuning in to your perceptions by visiting a public or school library. How does its collection appear to you?

_____

What do you like about the collection?

_____

What changes would you make if you were in charge?

_____

YOUR NEW SCHOOL

Although you have been to the school at least once for your interview and perhaps a few more times if you were called back and then visited the LMC after you got the job, you were probably too preoccupied to take much notice of your surroundings. But now that you are really in place as the SLMS and have some familiarity with your facility, it is time for you to explore the rest of the building.

A Sense of Place

Looking at the LMC as your home means the rest of the school is your neighborhood. If you had just moved into a new home, one of the first things you would do is walk around, finding out where the shops and restaurants are located. The same attitude should be present as you get comfortable in your building.

Stroll down the corridors and take note of what you see. If the school year is just beginning, the walls will not have any student work hanging, but you can still learn a great deal. Many elementary schools have signs expressing expected behaviors such as, "We do not say hurtful things to others." Do trophy cases in a high school have only cups and plaques from team sports, or do they also include awards for scholastic competitions? Is there a "Wall of Fame"? If so, who is honored? Are there student-produced murals? Is the school's mission statement displayed prominently? What is present and what is missing are indicators of the school's priorities.

Along your walk, identify key offices. In the elementary school, you should look for the nurse and reading teacher as well as any computer labs. At middle and high school levels, you should also find the guidance and subject department offices. See where the classrooms are for science, English, world languages, and so on. Learn whether the school has a radio or television studio. Where is the auditorium? It is definitely helpful to know where the cafeteria is located.

Take time to observe the numbering on doors and where restrooms for students and faculty are situated. Visitors to the building have a tendency to drop in at the LMC when lost and ask for directions. It is embarrassing to say that you are new and do not know.

A Walking Tour

What do you remember most about the school when you were there for the first time?

_____

Does it feel welcoming? Does it seem student centered?

_____

Are unspoken messages the same as the ones that are voiced?

_____

Secretaries and Custodians

It is time to smile and get to know the neighbors. Keep a pad tucked into your pocket so that you can make notes after you meet someone. Set a goal for yourself as to how much time you think you will need to become acquainted with your new community. In a small school you will become familiar with almost everyone in a short time. If you are in a middle or high school, you might need most of the year. Try to find a current yearbook. It will remind you of the names that go with the faces and the area of the school with which they are connected.

You probably have been told that you must make friends with the secretaries and custodians. While very true, do not look on this as a task to be checked off, but rather consider it an opportunity to become familiar with the people (along with aides and cafeteria staff) who are often the most underpaid in the district and who still give of themselves every day to take care of students and faculty. Focus on learning their names and one or two things about them to help you remember who they are as individuals. Keep your initial contacts brief. Everyone is busy, and you do not want to be a distraction. Build on these first connections throughout the year.

While secretaries are all part of the daytime staff, custodians work shifts. Although it is more difficult to meet those who start when the school day ends, pay particular attention to the one responsible for keeping the LMC clean. Since you will probably be staying late a few days each week, you will have plenty of chances to initiate conversations. Become familiar with his routines and note what is cleaned regularly and what rarely gets done.

When necessary, request rather than tell what you would like done. For example, you may have noticed that the computer area is very dusty. Many custodians hesitate to touch what they see as expensive equipment. You might chat with the custodian and ask if he would clean them. If he seems concerned, suggest that he can check with the lead custodian for appropriate supplies. Apologize (and sometimes help) when a party or celebration held in the LMC has created more than the usual mess. And *always* make a point of acknowledging the job that he does and how much you appreciate it.

Meeting Secretaries and Custodians

What information besides your name and job title will you offer when meeting secretaries and custodians?

_____

What two questions might you ask them?

_____

_____

Teachers

Chapter 6 will go into details about developing your connection with teachers, but first you must meet your colleagues. Use the early days to get a sense of the faculty. What is the ratio between tenured and nontenured staff? How diverse is the faculty in age and ethnicity? When a faculty's racial and ethnic balance mirror the town or area served by the school, there tends to be a good relationship with the community.

On a lighter note, check to see how teachers dress. The way you prepared for your interview may not fit with your new school. Overdressing is to be avoided as much as underdressing is. In most places, tailored corporate suits are too much. Sweats and jeans may be acceptable when getting rooms ready for the first day, but they can rarely be worn on a regular basis. Even if some teachers do so, aim for the middle or upper range rather than the bottom. Your clothing is another form of communication, and you want to be seen as a leader.

In most places teachers belong to a union, either the local affiliate of the National Education Association or the American Federation of Teachers. You will be asked to join and, unless you have strong feelings to the contrary, you should do so. Unions are not only responsible for improving the salary scale but also represent you if you are harassed by administrators or have other issues that affect your job.

If negotiations are under way, tensions tend to rise and job actions (including strikes) might be undertaken. Nontenured people usually do not take part in these, since the union tends to keep you from putting your job at risk. Your colleagues will understand. You can show your solidarity when the next contract rolls around. However, be prepared to see hostility shown to tenured faculty members who do not support the union. While some staff members continue the enmity afterward—particularly if there has been a strike—you still must get along with everyone.

Political beliefs can be equally delicate. The old adage of not discussing politics or religion is a good one to follow, at least until you are comfortable with the local culture. Some localities tolerate a wide disparity of opinion and debates without animosity. Other areas are distinctly liberal or conservative and question the intelligence of those who think otherwise. Tread cautiously.

Getting the Lay of the Land

Does the school have a diverse faculty or is it "white bread"? What does this suggest?

_____

What is the unwritten dress code?

_____

How do you feel about teachers' unions?

_____

Administrators

In chapter 7 you will learn how to create and nurture a positive relationship with your administrators. What is important now is making a second impression. Some time has passed since your job interview, and the principal has handled many other matters in the interim. You need to reestablish who you are and set the tone for the future.

Small schools tend to have a single administrator and informal collegiality is common. If all teachers address the principal by her first name, you can feel free to do so as well. However, wait until you are sure. The teachers might use a first name among themselves, but not when speaking directly to the principal. Sometimes only the long-term staff members have that privilege, and you definitely do not want to be presumptuous.

Whatever is the correct way of speaking with the principal and any other supervisors, be sure to greet them and acknowledge their presence. Do not hold them up to speak at length. Casual meetings are not the time for full-length conversations. If they stop and talk with you, pay full attention and do not try to hurry off unless there is a dire emergency (which you should immediately explain).

In a large school, you are likely to have a supervisor other than the principal, who will be a more distant contact. This person will be your major connection to the higher administration, so you want to get to know him well. Consider scheduling a weekly meeting time to make sure you are meeting expectations and get advice on changes that need to be made.

Principally Speaking

Who is your immediate supervisor?

_____

How long has this person been in this job? In the district?

_____

Are there other building-level administrators? Who are they?

_____

Students

Although they are your prime focus, you will not have much chance to meet students until the school year gets under way. As with other members of the educational community, use your observation skills first.

How do students walk through the halls? Notice whether there is a lot of pushing and shoving and how teachers react to it. Are the students loud? Their voice level is neither good nor bad if it is between classes, but is merely a clue to what is considered acceptable in the building. In middle and high schools there may be an issue with vulgar language. Depending on whether it exists and how long you have been out of school, this may be surprising and possibly uncomfortable for you. Once you have established yourself, you can let students know that using those words in your presence—even when not directed toward you—is not acceptable. If they have come to like and respect you, they will be careful. But you can expect them to slip and then apologize.

Observe the groups in corridors. This is the customary bonding time for students, and it pays to be aware of it. You may go along with the groups they prefer or break things up when you later create projects. Even in high school, you may see boys mostly with boys and girls with girls. Also notice whether they practice their own form of racial or ethnic segregation. Later you can discover what is at the root of it. Is it the way the neighborhood is, or is it an even more deeply ingrained prejudice? Once students are involved in team sports, a more natural integration takes place.

Is there an official dress code? Is it enforced? At middle and high schools you can frequently identify the various strata by the type of clothing worn. Jocks, student government leaders, technogeeks, skateboarders, drama types, and those devoted to the band have what might as well be their own uniforms. Develop a sense of how these groups are regarded. You will be trying to reach them all, but you should know how they fit within the student hierarchy.

See chapter 5, "Reaching Your Students," for more specific ways to nurture this vital connection.

Knowing Your Students

What are your expectations for student behavior?

What cliques and groups were there when you went to school? In which one were you?

How might that affect your reaction to your students?

Your Support Staff

The term *support staff* encompasses both paid and volunteer assistants in the LMC. Ordinarily, these would be the first people to get to know, but since many of you will have no support staff at all, this is being discussed last.

If you are among the fortunate who have paid clerical help, do everything you can to show your gratitude. Make sure your supervisor is aware of how the efforts of this person (or, if you are very lucky, these persons) are contributing to student achievement. You can point out every time they do something that improves efficiency, or how they have allowed you to spend more time with classes and individuals ensuring that important skills are learned.

Be sure the support staff are involved with and aware of the philosophy, vision, and mission for the SLMP. They need to feel the same sense of ownership you do. Acknowledge their achievements. As you are the one in charge, accept responsibility for any mistakes they might make. You should have been checking more closely. When they see you respect and protect them, they feel comfortable in letting you know when things are going wrong so you have a chance to avoid a disaster before it happens.

It is hard for intelligent people to do boring tasks such as shelving, straightening, and checking books in on a daily basis. To keep your support staff happy—and prevent them from leaving for something that pays better and is more interesting—find out what they like to do best and see how you can restructure their jobs so they have a chance to shine. Some people love to do displays. As long as you have frequent conversations about topics and what might be included in displays, give the job away. A few actually enjoy cataloging. Review what they do periodically and be available for conversations about the best classification or what subject headings to use. Before long you will have a paraprofessional rather than a clerk.

For those who depend on volunteers, the same advice holds true. You have to make them want to come to work in the LMC. If the tasks are too dreary, you will find them skipping their scheduled time and eventually drifting away. Give people ownership of specific tasks. Perhaps someone likes to mend books. Get pamphlets on the subject along with supplies. Put everything in a box with the person's name on it. Whenever she shows up, make sure she has some time to work on her project in addition to returning books to the shelves or whatever is generally expected.

In some schools, you have neither support staff nor volunteers. First determine if there is a policy discouraging the latter. Most schools now like parent involvement, but there are still some that try to keep them out. As long as there are no such restrictions, look for ways to recruit people.

Contact the parent-teacher organization's president and see if she can suggest some names of potential volunteers. With your principal's permission, send out letters inviting interested parties to a tea in the LMC. Inform attendees about the importance of the SLMP to student achievement and let them know that their efforts will give you more time to work with their children. Explain how much of a commitment they need to make. Perhaps you want them once a week for a morning or afternoon. Of course, more is always better. You might also tap local senior citizen groups for another source of help.

Realize that you will need to set aside time to train your volunteers. As they become comfortable in the LMC and learn more, many become interested in librarianship. Be prepared to help those who decide they want to make it their career, too.

Supporting Your Support Staff

Do you have clerical help? What is their schedule?

_____

If you have volunteers, who is the contact person?

_____

YOUR NEW DISTRICT AND COMMUNITY

With so much to do in your LMC and getting to know the people in your school, it seems an overwhelming thought to have to consider the district at large as well as the community. Nonetheless, limiting yourself to your building will keep you from perceiving why certain things happen or do not happen. Understanding how each part fits into the larger whole gives you a point of reference as to how to go about making changes and anticipating what will fly and what will not.

The District

By now you should be aware of the size of your school district. You should know how many schools it has and what grade levels they serve. Find out how to reach out to the other SLMSs in the district. Some districts have regular meetings, with an administrator or one of the librarians being in charge. In other places there are informal, irregularly scheduled get-togethers.

If there is nothing in place, you should still make every effort to get in touch with your colleagues in the district. These people are your best sources for information on library procedures. Although there are always differences from building to building, they can tell you what jobbers they use, if an information literacy curriculum is in place, and how purchase orders are handled. In other words, they can give you the inside details on the nitty-gritty of your job.

Get their e-mail addresses and send out a message. Even if you cannot meet in person for a while, it is good to have someone you can ask for help. Since you are the one looking for guidance, you might suggest meeting them at their LMC before or after school.

Although your contact with the central administration will be minimal (aside from accounts payable and perhaps payroll), you should be aware of who the superintendent of schools is and the roles and names of the various assistant superintendents, as well as any district-level coordinators. On occasion, they may want to use your facility either after or during school hours, and it is wise to know who they are. When they do appear in the LMC, introduce yourself, offer to help in any way necessary, and then occupy yourself in a manner that shows your efficiency and competence.

You should also have some knowledge of board of education members. Occasionally they are volunteers in your LMC. In some districts they have the run of the place and will come strolling into your facility. You get to recognize these drop-ins quickly. Greet them, ask if they need anything, and then continue to do your work. When you get to know them better, you may have lengthier conversations, but *never* talk negatively about anyone in the building. Nothing is ever confidential and word will get back.

Knowing Your District

What do you know about your school district?

_____

Which people do you need to contact?

_____

The Community

No matter how large a school district is, it is still only part of the community. Budgets get passed or voted down based on how residents feel about education and the manner in which it is handled in their town or city. People's values also influence what happens in the schools. Controversies over issues such as intelligent design, sex education, and school prayer affect teaching.

The SLMP is often a target of various ideologies. The ALA's Office for Intellectual Freedom has reported a continuing increase in the number of titles challenged by community members. While chapter 4 discusses how to manage challenges, you need to have a sense of your community in order to know where the greatest weight of opinion is. If your philosophy is severely at odds with local values, you will find yourself either acting in ways you do not approve or in confrontation with angry parents.

If you live where you work, you are aware of how people feel. An outsider has to do some research to understand the forces that govern the community. One simple method is to get the local newspaper for a few weeks. Check the editorials and the letters. Read featured stories to see what slant is taken. In a short time, you will have learned the names of the more influential residents and know what is valued.

Community Contact

What are the major businesses in the community?

_____

What issues are engaging people's attention?

_____

THE CULTURE OF THE EDUCATIONAL COMMUNITY

Administrators come and go at the building and district level. Some are liked and others are heartily despised. They all promise a change, and to some extent they keep their word. Under the guidance of the best of them, things improve. But all too often, after an initial turnaround, the situation returns to its familiar ways. What goes wrong?

Any organization, whether it is a corporation, a school district, or even a town, has its own culture. One community values its historical heritage, and civic pride is a cornerstone for decision making. Another town has a low regard for education, accepting it as a grim necessity, and votes down school budgets as a matter of course. In different schools the focus is on being innovative, or perhaps it is on being viewed as the best.

No matter who is in charge, these attitudes remain the same. If you want to make changes, you will have to do so by framing your ideas so they are aligned with the existing culture. Once more, you need to see whether your philosophy is a comfortable fit within this educational community.

Cultural Considerations

How would you describe the culture of your new school or district?

_____

Does this mesh easily with your philosophy? If not, is it workable?

_____

Key Ideas

- Trust yourself—you know more about your job than the administrators or teachers do.
- The LMC's physical arrangement can work for or against you.
- Weed the collection the first year only if the situation is critical.
- Make the facility fit your philosophy.
- Tour the school building to see the face it presents to the world.
- In getting to know secretaries and custodians, take a real interest in them.
- Note to what extent faculty diversity reflects the community.
- Discover the power of the local union and strongly consider joining.
- Start early in developing your relationship with your immediate supervisor.
- Know whether there is a dress code and, if so, how it is enforced.
- Nurture your volunteers; the rewards are great.
- Your school does not exist in a vacuum; it is an integral part of the district and community.
- Get to know the other SLMSs in the district. They are your lifeline.
- Become familiar with the names and jobs of those in the central administration.
- Board of education members may drop in at the LMC. Handle them carefully.
- Determine the culture of the educational community.

CHAPTER 4

Getting Yourself Organized

If there were any more pages to read, it would need an ISBN.

Policies
- Selection Policy
- Acceptable Use Policy
- Handbooks

Your Schedule
- Rigid Schedules
- Flexible Schedules

Your Facility
- Student-Friendly Environment
- Teacher Area
- Floor Plan

Purchase Orders
- Print and Electronic Materials
- Supplies and Other Items
- Processing Materials

Your Office
- Resources
- File Cabinets

*I*n the days before school starts and during the first week or so while things are relatively calm, take time to settle into your new environment and make it your own. This will be *your space,* reflecting your personality and philosophy. You need to find out what you have inherited, determine what can stay and what should be tossed, and identify and locate any missing resources.

POLICIES

You should understand the difference between policies and guidelines. Policies are procedures passed by the school board. Many school library media specialists write their own guidelines for various aspects of their job, but without board approval, these have no force. However, they are helpful in suggesting the way the LMC operates, and you may want to see if you can, at some future date, submit them to the board and turn them into policies.

Selection Policy

The most important (and frequently nonexistent) document that you need is a selection policy. Although you see yourself as responsible for new acquisitions, technically you are functioning as an agent of the school board, and you should be operating under a policy it has approved. If you have a selection policy previously passed by the board, make sure it has been updated to include electronic resources. In the event that such guidelines drawn up by a previous SLMS but never submitted for passage exist, it is crucial that you draft one that becomes a legal document and acts as a safety net for every decision you make in building your collection.

As you probably recall from your library school classes, the selection policy covers how you choose material for the collection, as well as the course of action that begins when someone challenges an item. Remember that no one, not even the superintendent of schools, can remove a title from the collection simply because a concern has been raised. While this is not the same as discarding books when you weed, that process should also be detailed in the selection policy.

In developing the document, you will want to work with the other SLMSs in the district, since this policy is not limited to a particular school. By now you know who is responsible for supervising the SLMSs.

Approach that person and suggest that a committee of three or four develop a draft to be approved by the entire group before being sent to the board.

The best place to start creating that draft is by going to the Office for Intellectual Freedom's web page (http://www.ala.org/oif/). Click on "Challenge Support," then on "Dealing with Challenges." Scroll down to "Workbook for Selection Policy Writing." The information is free and comprehensive. It will guide you through all the components of a selection policy, and it gives examples for the various sections as well as a complete sample policy. Although the workbook is listed under "Dealing with Challenges" on the website, it is imperative that you have a selection policy in place *before* there is any "Request for Reconsideration."

Having a book or other library resource challenged is the biggest nightmare for any SLMS, and even more so for one new to the profession or the school. Too often the fear of this possibility leads to self-censorship which deprives students of their right to access information. It is far better to act as a professional, be prepared with a policy that will support you, and recognize that there is a true difference between selection and censorship.

Selection looks at a work in its entirety and seeks to determine whether the content meets the philosophy, mission, and objectives of the school and the SLMP. The SLMS takes into account whether the reading, interest, and emotional levels of a work are appropriate for the intended grade range (materials are not chosen for a single grade). *Censorship,* by contrast, focuses on bits and pieces within the whole as the basis for rejection.

Once you have an approved selection policy in place, you can deal with daily issues as well as a crisis with equanimity. Having the basis for making acquisitions in writing helps you deal with teachers who request items that do not meet the policy's criteria, such as purchasing a video that has not been reviewed or previewed. The policy also serves as a guide when a parent wishes to donate thirty years of *National Geographic* magazines and wants a statement of their value for income tax purposes.

Obviously, the policy is most critical when someone wants to have an item removed from the LMC. What happens next depends on a number of factors. If you are the first to hear of the complaint, do not overreact. Start with the assumption that the claim has validity. You will then be more likely to treat the person with a level of respect that will help the process go forward with the least possible confrontational behavior. Inform the complainant that you will notify the administration immediately so that the established procedures can be followed. Then take a deep calming breath and review the selection policy *before* speaking to your principal so that you can clearly remind her of the steps that must be followed.

On occasion, administrators are approached first by a complainant. If you have not been proactive in ensuring that they are familiar with the selection policy, they may pull the item to forestall the complaint. In that case, take a few more deep breaths. Let the administrators know that you understand their concern, but as there is a policy in place, they can allow the process to proceed in a manner that respects the sensibilities of the challenger while protecting the rights of *all* students.

Know that you have access to support during this stressful time. Your state library association probably has an intellectual freedom chair who should be notified. In addition, you can and should call or fax the Office for Intellectual Freedom. You can fax information to 312-280-4227. They will be happy to assist you and provide a wealth of helpful material. You can also reach the office via e-mail at oif@ala.org.

In the event a person or group wants to remove items from your collection and you do not yet have a selection policy in place, the Office for Intellectual Freedom will be able to advise you. You can download the workbook even at this late date and suggest to administrators that by following its recommendations, the district can handle the complaint without appearing to be censors.

Intellectual Freedom Issues

When was your selection policy last updated? What if anything is missing?

_____

Characterize your school district's openness to intellectual freedom.

_____

What in the "Workbook for Selection Policy Writing" did you find most surprising?

_____

Do you think you can select materials without self-censoring?

_____

What is the first thing to say to a parent who is challenging a book?

_____

Acceptable Use Policy

An acceptable use policy (AUP) delineates what is permitted and what is prohibited when accessing the Internet and sending e-mail, and it stipulates other protocols and etiquette in using the network. The consequences for violating any of these stipulations should be clearly spelled out in the policy. Generally, in order for students to be permitted to use school computers, they and their parents or guardians must both sign the document. Make time to read through the policy so that you will be familiar with all of its requirements and prohibitions.

If your district does not have an AUP, you should explore the possibility of adding one as soon as possible. Locate a number of samples before drafting your own. Begin by looking locally. The school library association in your state is likely to have an electronic discussion list for members which you can query for examples of AUPs.

An Internet search will reveal those in use in various schools around the country. Be wary before adopting them, however, since many have been hanging around for up to ten years and deal with issues that no longer exist, while ignoring other issues that have emerged in the intervening time.

Try to contact the SLMSs in the other schools in your district. See if they have been using any guidelines in their buildings. Ask if they would like to work with you in crafting the wording for an AUP to send to the board.

As you review the examples, you may be surprised to see what restrictions different schools impose. You probably expect that most schools prohibit students from going into chat rooms, but it may be startling to find that many do not permit student e-mail. Their concern is a matter of security and lawsuits.

Security is a particular issue for the technology department (whether it is a single person or a sizable group), which is responsible for the integrity of the network. The big fear is a virus getting into the system, and most come by way of e-mail. No matter how many warnings are sent out about not opening suspect documents, inevitably someone fails to follow these instructions. Many schools operate on the belief that students are more careless than adults, and so prohibit them from accessing e-mail. If *you* are the technology department, follow past practices until you determine whether changes need to be made and the best way to get them in place.

School boards are very careful about exposing themselves to potential litigation, and they can be held liable for a defamatory e-mail sent on a school computer. (Some districts do not permit students to create websites for the same reason.) Students find this very frustrating, since they like to send their homework to themselves and print the hard copy on a school printer, particularly if theirs is not functioning for some reason.

Even staff often have some limitations placed on their use of the network. Teachers may be permitted to use their personal e-mail, but frequently they are restricted to the school's network. Consider helping students by having them send their needed homework to an address at the LMC which you can access. If this does not become too time-consuming, you can do printouts in the morning, letting the students pick theirs up before school starts.

Be prepared to help teachers with e-mail. While most now use it in school and at home, a handful of computer-wary souls have been trying to avoid dealing with this form of communication. When an administrator decides that henceforth all memos and messages will be sent electronically, they panic. Quietly guiding them through the process may be the start of a relationship leading to future collaboration.

Even regular users may encounter difficulties with the idiosyncrasies—or malfunctions—of the district's system. As the most easily reached technology and information expert, you are the one to whom they may bring their woes, anger, and frustration. Be as helpful as you can without making negative comments about the technology department.

Network Necessities

According to the AUP, what privileges do users get?

_____

What restrictions are listed in the AUP?

_____

Are the consequences for violating the AUP similar to the penalties for mishandling print material?

_____

What changes would you make in the AUP if you could?

_____

Handbooks

High schools and many middle schools give students handbooks. These sometimes come in the form of a planner with vacations and other important dates noted. The format will usually include the school philosophy, mission, and perhaps a listing of the sports and clubs available. The handbook will also spell out school rules and the consequences for violating them. Some handbooks offer helpful advice for keeping organized and being successful academically.

Teachers may get a handbook similar to what the students received, with added information about marking periods and possibly directives about attendance. At all levels, the faculty receives numerous other documents. However these are arranged, it is important for you to go through them to know what they contain.

Among the many documents will be statements about student privacy, and possibly limits on what outside materials may be used in class. Look for policy numbers on these documents to alert you to the fact that they carry the weight of the board behind them. Some districts distribute information on copyright so they are not implicated if teachers violate it, knowingly or not. You may also find items giving state laws on various topics.

While not as weighty, the procedures for taking professional or sick days are nevertheless important and are generally among the papers you will receive. You should check for information on how to get your e-mail account if you have not yet been given one. Make a copy of the list of faculty members in the school. If the form omits it, find out what department or grade they teach and note it next to their names. Slip it into your desk drawer to help you remember everyone.

As you skim through the documents, put a flag or sticky note on the ones you want to review in more detail at a later date. These may include your job description and procedures for observations and evaluations. Put a binder or booklet containing all the documents in a place where you will remember it. Although you may rarely consult it during the school year, you don't want to be hunting frantically for it when you need to find a particular item.

Paperwork

How many policy documents were included in your handbook?

_____

Are there any unexpected items in your job description?

_____

What clues to your school can be found in the documents you received?

_____

YOUR SCHEDULE

Whether rigid or flexible, your schedule will affect how you interact with teachers and students. It should reflect your philosophy as much as possible. Although you cannot change a rigid schedule, you should seek approaches that build your connections with teachers and the classroom. Thinking this through, even though you will probably make adjustments as you go along, will help keep you from feeling pulled in all directions as the year begins.

Rigid Schedules

Most elementary and some middle schools schedule classes into the LMC so that classroom teachers can have their prep periods, that is, contractual periods set aside to attend to classroom-related tasks. In such cases, teachers will drop off and pick up their classes at your door according to the fixed or rigid schedule which you receive along with the other papers you are given on your first day. Some SLMSs are assigned to multiple buildings and will need to work around that as well. Analyze your situation now for clues as to how you will be structuring your time.

How often do you see each class? It is hard to have continuity when students only come once a week. If you see them less frequently, you will need to be even more conscientious about reminding them of what they learned the previous time. Consider ending each session with a list of highlights of the lesson even if you have to identify them yourself. Then review these when the class returns.

Do students from the same grade level follow each other, or do you jump from a kindergarten class to fourth grade and back to second? In the latter case, you have many preparations for the same day. Determine which works best for you—making plans on a daily basis or doing them all at once for the entire week. You will want to present the same lesson for all students at a given grade level—with some modification depending on whether you get special requests from teachers.

Look to see how you can build openings within your schedule. Perhaps you have a slot a few days a week when *all* students can come to return books and check out new ones. If you have volunteers, you will want to have a number of them in at that time. This will keep your lessons from being chopped up by book selection.

Cross-check your schedule with the school calendar. How many days in the year will you see each class? Are adjustments made for vacations, or do those students miss coming to the LMC? You may be surprised to see how little contact time you have with them.

Start thinking of how you will present the curriculum within the allotted periods. Remember not to limit a lesson to a single skill. Information literacy requires students, whatever their level, to learn how to combine several skills in order to meet their research needs. It is better to focus on what you want them to be able to do by the end of a marking period, and create inquiry-based units that build toward that end.

Flexible Schedules

SLMSs in high schools, most middle schools, and a lucky few in elementary schools have open or flexible schedules, which are based solely on teacher requests or curriculum requirements. While this is the most effective way to achieve the mission of the SLMP, making it happen is your responsibility. You will have to be proactive in reaching teachers, selling your program, and ensuring that all students have frequent opportunities to become information-literate.

Chapter 6, "Reaching Your Teachers," will give you ideas on how to create a climate for collaboration on joint teaching projects. However, with the school year just beginning, you will need to move quickly to be sure that you have at least scheduled your orientations. At the middle and high school levels, you want to contact all English teachers for the entering class (most often, sixth and ninth grades) and ask them when they would like to bring their classes to the LMC. For elementary students, you may need to do orientations with everyone.

If at all possible, ask these teachers for the topic of their opening unit and use it as an example in your orientation. Alert them to your plans and offer to schedule two days in the LMC. Having students apply the information you presented will help them remember it as the year progresses.

Just as with rigidly scheduled SLMSs, you should review the curriculum. Try to determine which subject areas best connect with the skills you are to teach. You will need to make the appropriate connections to be sure that you can cover what is required. In some cases, you may want to meet with supervisors or department chairs to help you plan better.

Assessing Your Schedule

If you are rigidly scheduled, identify your greatest challenges.

_____

What are one or two things you can do to manage these challenges?

_____

If you are flexibly scheduled, what will be your first steps to bring in classes?

_____

YOUR FACILITY

In your initial visits you looked around the LMC and made some judgments about it. Now that you are the one in charge, it is time to take a closer look to see what you can do to make the place yours.

Student-Friendly Environment

Review what you said in the last chapter about the message the LMC was sending. Consider what simple action steps you can take to make the room more inviting.

One of the easiest changes to make is to highlight student achievement. At the secondary school level, you can devote a wall to newspaper accounts relating to the school. Athletes are regularly featured. Cut out the articles and paste them onto a poster board mounted in a prominent location. Look for other accomplishments as well. Academic competition teams get less coverage, but when they make great showings, it is usually reported. Individuals are occasionally highlighted for community service or other special activities. In some areas, one or more students has a column in the local paper which can also be posted.

Another way of featuring students is to exhibit their work in the LMC. Were any examples displayed when you made your first visit to the school? In that case, at least some teachers are likely to continue to bring you student creations. If not, you will need to invite them to use your facility to showcase what has occurred in their classes.

At all grade levels, the art teachers are the best source for student work. They usually focus on decorating the school, but you can encourage them to do the same for the LMC. Remind them that meetings are often held in your room, and early arrivals spend more time looking at what is on display than do people who walk through the halls to get to their destinations.

When you work with classes during the year, see if teachers will send culminating projects to the LMC. This not only acknowledges students but is also an incentive for other teachers to work with you. If there is a school newsletter that goes to parents, be sure to add a piece—with pictures—about which classes have their work on exhibit. Invite parents in to view the display.

Check out the magazine collection. Students love to leaf through magazines. Sometimes SLMSs cancel titles when faced with budget cuts, but magazines are an important avenue for recreational reading, particularly for those who show little interest in books.

How many periodicals do you have that really appeal to students? Consider asking them what should be added—or deleted. Chapter 5 suggests techniques for building that relationship. Giving students a say in what materials are ordered will enhance the collection's appeal.

Don't neatly shelve all your magazines. High schools usually have a lounge area near this collection. Place some titles on a small nearby table. In lower grades, use the tops of low bookcases. At the primary level, put magazines on the tilt-top picture book tables.

Since students are most attracted to the computer area, think of ways to further utilize this section. Promote the website of the week or a new search engine to explore. (Perhaps they will discover the world beyond Google.) Select a few new books or interesting older ones and arrange them with a catchy slogan. At the high school level, advertise club meetings or the formation of a new club. Whatever you do, change it at least weekly. Students' attention span is short, and they stop noticing things that are around too long.

Teacher Area

Think of what you can do to make teachers comfortable in the LMC. The more time they spend there without their students, the greater the likelihood that they will discover what the SLMP has to offer. That makes them more open to working collaboratively with you.

Much of what is possible depends on the size of your facility. Look for creative solutions. If you have study carrels, label one or two for teacher use. Teachers appreciate a quiet space in which to work. Place a small "Reserved for Teachers" sign on a table to serve the same purpose. You can always remove it when the LMC is very busy.

If you get some magazines that teachers enjoy, place them in the designated teacher area. At the high school level you can also put out a few of your newer mysteries or other adult-level titles. Keep a supply of pens and paper for them to use when they are in the LMC. Teachers are invariably grateful when someone does something special for them.

Floor Plan

Stand in various places in the room. How well can you see students from these positions? Where are the blind spots?

The arrangement of the room can help or hinder your ability to maintain discipline. Students are aware when they are visible and are less likely to get into mischief when they know you can see them easily. However, no library is free from hidden areas.

The best possible arrangement is to have tall book stacks ringing the room and display-height shelving on the floor area. Few facilities have the luxury of that much space. Recognize that you will need to check locations where students are out of your normal line of sight. Special mirrors can be installed to help you.

Are any areas of the LMC hard to spot? Is there a collection, such as graphic novels, that you would like to feature? Either by making your own signs or getting help from the graphic arts department, you can better identify these sections without spending much money.

Are all tables and chairs in one place so that multiple classes intermingle? You want to minimize that as much as possible. See if furniture can be repositioned to create some separation. Note that circular tables not only take up more floor space, they also promote socializing. If you have too many round tables, you might want to think about exchanging them for rectangular ones available elsewhere in the building or district. Purchasing new furniture has significant budget implications and, unless it had been planned for, is impossible during your first year.

Creating Your Place

What can you do to make your LMC inviting to students and faculty?

_____

What are the room's best features?

_____

What are the worst ones, and what can you do in the short term to minimize them?

_____

PURCHASE ORDERS

Now that you have some ideas of what to do with the reading room floor, it is time to turn to your office area. Locate the purchase orders (POs) for this and previous school years. In large LMCs they will probably be kept in three-ring binders; smaller LMCs may keep them in a file cabinet. You will be returning to them when you work on your budget (see chapter 9), but at the moment all you are doing is getting a sense of what is coming in.

If your predecessor was kind enough to leave you a spreadsheet of the POs, pull it up as you go over the items; otherwise create one. You are looking to see how books and electronic materials are acquired, what newspapers and magazines have been purchased and from where, what sources are used for library supplies, and what funds are expended for technical and professional purposes.

Print and Electronic Materials

SLMSs usually purchase the bulk of their books from a jobber. Jobbers are like wholesale bookstores, which means you do not have to send orders to individual publishers. Among the more common ones are Baker and Taylor, Brodart, and Follett. Until you have had a chance to explore further, stick with the company the previous SLMS used.

Jobbers have your processing specifications on file, and you are not ready to make any changes here. These specifications include cataloging choices (F or FIC, number of letters under the Dewey Decimal number, etc.), where book pockets and spine label are placed, and what kind of covers you want for paperbacks. If your LMC is automated, this also means bar codes are placed according to the preference for your LMC and a data disk (or online downloading of records) is sent so that new materials can be quickly entered into the catalog. If you have a security system, you may also request detection tags to be placed in books.

Note that jobbers give you a discount, but these are not uniform. Trade books have the greatest reduction, while you receive only 10 percent off library bound titles. Professional books are frequently sold at list price.

If you do want to consider another jobber at a future date, copy a PO and send it to one or more different vendors minus the discount and net pricing information. You will find that you might be able to save significant money this way. However, cost is not the only reason to make a change. Look at the previous POs to see how many titles were back ordered or canceled. While it is recommended that you over-order, putting "do not exceed amount" to allow for items no longer in stock, you want to be sure that all your funds are expended. If it takes too long to get everything, the order may be closed out by your accounts payable department and you will lose access to money previously allocated to the LMC.

Check for other book purchases. Orders for encyclopedias, atlases, and major reference titles are most often sent directly to the publisher, even at the elementary level. Middle and high schools do even more direct purchases. You will see POs for ABC-CLIO, Facts On File, and Gale, among others.

Some SLMSs use local vendors as well. These publisher's representatives sell material from a number of houses and can be marvelous resources over time. The reputable ones know your collection and your student body. They make excellent recommendations, help you to avoid duplicate ordering, and give you an opportunity to get books on your shelves quicker as they alert you to titles before publication. Sometimes you can acquire these titles at special pricing. You still get discounts; local vendors often prepare the orders for you to attach to your PO and add a personal touch to the book-buying process. Since they generally bring books for you to look at, you can often invite teachers to participate in your purchasing decisions.

Most schools also use a jobber for magazines. EBSCO and W. T. Cox are among the larger ones, but there are a number of smaller vendors. Again, you do not want to make any changes as yet (and you might be very happy with the one you have), although some districts put the list of subscriptions out to bid each year. Unfortunately, if you switch companies, you may miss some issues in the process.

Obviously, a periodical jobber saves you the insanity of keeping track of what can be an extensive list of titles. You can ignore all the letters reminding you to resubscribe. At the appropriate time—usually in the early spring, but it can be after the district budget has been certified— you send your list with any additions or deletions to your vendor. All magazines then start at the same time, simplifying your life.

High schools and some middle schools also receive newspapers. This can be a nightmare if you do not have a good supplier. Sometimes it is simpler to find a student who has a paper route and can deliver to the LMC. Be sure that you are getting both national and local papers. If ethnic papers are available in your area, look into getting a subscription.

Your online databases may be purchased directly, obtained through the state, or via a consortium to which you belong. Other than state-supplied resources, you will find POs for what you are getting in your LMC. As these change somewhat from year to year, you will want to check back and see if there have been any adjustments.

Be sure that any new electronic resources have been received and are accessible. Depending on your school, they will be accessed either on the website, from computer desktops, or from whatever the technology department has set up. (Don't forget to remove any databases that have been dropped.) Find out which ones you obtain for free either from your state or a consortium. Knowing which databases you get without cost helps you make decisions on future acquisitions.

Print and Electronic Acquisitions

What jobbers are you using for books and magazines?

_____

What proportion of your budget is used for books? Electronic databases? Magazines?

_____

Does the balance seem appropriate to you? What changes, if any, do you think should be considered?

_____

Supplies and Other Items

Where do you get your supplies? Brodart, Demco, Gaylord, and Highsmith are the biggest library supply houses. Their catalogs are filled with almost everything needed to run the LMC, from bookends and spine labels to signs and circulation desks. You can come up with a great wish list just by flipping through the pages.

Again, one company tends to get all or most of a school's business. In larger districts, a bid process is used to select the vendor. Sometimes a state contract allows you to choose another company without going out to bid. You will need to find out what the procedure is for your situation and follow it carefully.

General supplies such as construction paper, scissors, and tissues may be acquired from another company. You will need to check POs to see if you can identify where these items come from in your school. If you cannot figure it out, speak with a secretary or with other SLMSs in the district.

Computer and copier supplies are another issue. Ink for printers and toner for copiers are expensive. You will go through reams of paper at an alarming rate. Who pays for these items? Where are they obtained? It is different in each district, and you will need to learn what is done in yours.

Look for POs for various technical support and services. If your LMC is automated, there is an annual licensing agreement. Does the licensing fee come out of your budget or does the district pay for it? Do you have a maintenance agreement for copiers (and how do you call for repairs)? You will also have a contract to cover the servicing of any LMC security system.

Check to see if POs from the previous year show any reimbursements for professional days. Do they include registration at conferences? Was any money allowed for meals and travel? If you don't find anything, it may be because it comes out of the school budget. Alternatively, you may not get paid for conferences and everything comes out of your pocket. In some schools, you are not permitted any release time to attend out-of-district professional meetings. You will need to ask the secretary or the principal about this at a later date.

Your spreadsheet giving you an overview of what is ordered and with whom you will be dealing should be complete by now, although you never know what you might find. When you review the POs to create your budget for the next school year, it will not be as overwhelming because you will be familiar with the acquisition process.

Supplies and Sundries

Name some sources used for supplies in your LMC.

_____

What licensing and maintenance contracts did you find?

_____

What proportion of your budget goes to support LMC operations?

_____

Processing Materials

Library schools never spend any time discussing how you handle incoming materials, and yet, if you do not have clerical help, this is a time-consuming aspect of your job. Remember that you are responsible for promptly informing the accounts payable department that you have received what was on the POs so that vendors can be paid.

As books and supplies are unpacked, they need to be checked against the POs. Note what has come in and highlight or circle any missing items. Check with the vendor to see if these items are being shipped at a later date, have been overlooked, or are canceled. Be sure you are receiving all magazines and newspapers. Obviously, you sign off on these as soon as you have received one issue, since you are not going to hold the PO until the end of the school year. For new electronic databases, wait until they are up and running before you request payment for them.

Find out the procedure for informing accounts payable that you have received the items. Your signature is usually required, and you will probably have to include the date. Sometimes you are expected to indicate that it is OK to pay. To whom do you send these? What copy do you keep? If there is none for you, make one on the photocopier. In larger schools, separate your paid POs from those still not complete.

Ask what you do with incomplete orders. For significant amounts there generally is a procedure for partial payment. If you are confused or uncertain about how to do any of this, make an appointment with the school secretary or the accounts payable clerk, who will be happy to review the process with you. It is far simpler to talk you through it than to have to clean up mistakes.

Although most—if not all—of your books will come processed, they are not quite shelf-ready. They need to be stamped with the LMC name (check for a property stamp) and may have other information noted, such as the date of purchase, on the copyright page. If you do not have a clerk or experienced volunteers, check titles on the shelf to see where to stamp and write. Flip through the book to see if any interior pages should be stamped.

Review the classifications to be sure you agree with them. Occasionally a fiction title is placed in 813.54. Perhaps you want sports biographies filed with the sport rather than in biography. You will need to identify which titles you want in reference and, if you use them, determine if a special label should be applied for genre fiction. Many schools put a colored dot or a sticker on titles to be placed on a New Books shelf. Any changes which affect where items are permanently shelved must be noted on the record, whether electronic or print. You should also quickly check all books to ensure they are not damaged and have no upside-down pages.

Knowing the Process

To whom do you send checked-off POs?

_____

What information is entered into books in your collection?

_____

YOUR OFFICE

Whether you have a separate room or just a desk, a file cabinet, and some bookshelves, your office is your personal space. In cleaning up and going through what has been left by the previous SLMS, you will add to what you know about your new position. Then you can bring in whatever makes you feel comfortable when you sit down to work.

Resources

Go through the books on the shelf. You should find numerous resources such as the *Sears List of Subject Headings, Information Power: Building Partnerships for Learning,* and other professional literature. Review what is there and check copyright dates. Do not hang on to multiple editions of the same bibliographical resource. Those that are more than five years old should be considered for discard. Other titles may be old but still valid; see what they contain. If you have them available, put colored dots on any you think might be out-of-date. At the end of the year, review the ones you marked and decide what can be thrown out.

Look for items specific to the school and district. Among these might be curriculum guides for different subject areas as well as one for the SLMP, a technology plan, and, in a high school, the most recent accrediting report. You should have catalogs from vendors stored either on a shelf or in a file. Should you be unable to locate them or want one that is not on hand, go online and request it. Add dates to the corner of the covers (e.g., 9/07), since companies do not always put this information in an easy-to-spot location. Knowing when you received a catalog is a guide as to when it should be discarded.

See if you can locate manuals. You absolutely need to have the one for your library management system if your LMC is automated. It is also helpful to have manuals for copiers and printers, since you are invariably the one to do preliminary repairs.

High school and some middle school LMCs also have a file of yearbooks. These are invaluable for you. You can put faces to names and know who belongs in which department. You can also learn what sports and academic teams are available to students, as well as what clubs are part of the extracurricular activities. (Find out the procedure for circulating yearbooks. Alumni and others frequently want to borrow them, and they are irreplaceable.)

File Cabinets

Going through the file cabinets can be either a treasure hunt or an archaeological dig. Old memos and reports give fascinating insights into what has gone before. Some districts require accountings for professional days taken. If any of these are in the file, they give you a picture of what the previous SLMS attended.

Hang on to monthly and annual reports for the last five years. Older ones can be tossed. Those saved will help you compare and contrast your achievements. If they include statistics—not just circulation, but numbers of classes, types of reference questions, and so on—you can use them to build longitudinal data.

Articles from old magazines can be discarded, but they may give you a laugh to see what was considered important. Summer reading lists can also be dumped if they are not recent. If there are any from the last few years, keep them and realize that you will be expected to compile one.

Occasionally you can find a floor plan of the LMC in one of the files. This is definitely valuable and you will want to hold on to it. Invariably, the furniture placement is not what you currently have on the floor. However, the dimensions will help if you want to make changes in the future or merely create a library map for an orientation class.

Much of what you find in the file cabinets can be discarded, but it is fun and informative to go through them. You will be glad your predecessor left so much behind. After getting rid of the outdated and the superfluous, you will have plenty of space to begin your own collection. Your successor will appreciate it.

Creating Your Space

What important resources did you find in your office?

_____

Are you missing any key professional titles? What are they?

_____

What valuable items did you find in the file cabinets?

_____

Key Ideas

- Policies are school board-approved procedures.
- Be proactive in making administrators aware of the procedures in the selection policy.
- Use the ALA's Office for Intellectual Freedom as a resource.
- Check to see if your district or school has an AUP and become familiar with it.
- Review the student handbook and all information distributed to faculty.
- Look for simple ways to make the LMC more student-friendly.
- Analyze your schedule so you can organize your school year.
- Flexible schedules require you to be proactive in reaching teachers.
- Small changes to the facility can make students and teachers feel welcome there.
- Rearranging furniture can make the LMC more efficient and easier to manage.
- Jobbers and library supply houses simplify acquisitions.
- Know how to sign off on a PO.
- Learn the procedure for processing new books.
- Explore what was left behind in your office to learn more about your job, school, and district.

CHAPTER 5

Reaching Your Students

If they are so computer oriented, why don't they come with a manual?

No matter what you consider the challenges of your job, your first thoughts should always be about your students. They are the reason you are there. Unless you show them how important you consider their success, make friends with them, and let them know you are available if problems arise, you will not be fulfilling your mission.

START WITH A SMILE

The simplest way to make a connection is to smile. It will go a long way to putting both you and students at ease. For the ones just starting or new to a school, those first days are scary. A friendly face is a comforting sight, making them feel safe and encouraging them to get to know you better. Even at the upper grades, students respond easily to that silent greeting.

Ask about their summer and be ready to share some details of yours. Talk about any books they read and enjoyed, and suggest any related titles you know. The dialogue is a natural one and opens communication that will deepen over time. Keep in mind that your goal is for them to always see you as a source of nonjudgmental help.

Keep that smile going as the year progresses. While a welcoming face is easy to present on the first day or week of school, weariness sets in over time. With daily pressures or worrisome details on your mind, it is sometimes easy to forget that students are your first priority. Even more than adults, they will reflect the attitude you bring to them. Smile and show them you are glad to see them, no matter what else is happening.

THE POWER OF NAMES

Build on that opening connection by showing students that they are your main focus. One way to demonstrate that you care about each one is to learn their names so that you can greet them in the hall (be sure to always look pleasant as you walk down the corridors, regardless of what problems you may be juggling) or as they drop by to return a book or ask for assistance. This task is somewhat easier for those elementary-level SLMSs with rigid schedules who have class lists, but even if you are at a middle or high school, you should do your best to know students' names.

Although this can't be accomplished overnight, a good way to begin is to try to have short conversations with individuals and train your memory to recall something about each one to connect to their names. Many principals recognize the importance of this connection. If they are able to greet each student personally, so can you.

It is difficult, with all the other things you must do, to try to remember hundreds of identities, but that is a key to building relationships, and everyone will be very pleased that you have taken the trouble to know them. At the high school, this is vital because your students will be much more responsive once they see that you look on them as individuals and not just as one of a group. At the same time, they will show you their regard and look on you quite differently.

BUILDING RESPECT

One of the keys to successful interactions with students is to create a climate of mutual respect. You must give it in order to get it. Friendliness, courtesy, and consideration set a tone that brings large returns.

Those magical words from kindergarten—"please" and "thank you"—should consistently be present when you speak with students. As you help them or ask a question, pretend you are addressing a faculty member. The same courtesy you give to adults must be inherent in your dealings with students. You will know you are successful when you hear them use those words when speaking with you.

Be prepared to apologize. You might accidentally blame the wrong student or overreact because you are having a bad day. Acknowledge your mistake. Having adults say they are sorry teaches students that anyone can make an error, but it is important to own up to the responsibility for it.

If you do not have a plan for handling interruptions by staff members, you are likely to cut off the student with a few short words and turn to the adult. The message is quite clear as to which person is your priority. At a minimum, the courteous behavior is to excuse yourself, but you should go much further.

Tell the teacher or administrator that you will be back in a moment. Bring the conversation with the student to some sort of completion by giving a few directions as to how to proceed, indicating what to do in case a problem emerges, and saying when you will get back to the discussion. Have the student check in with you before leaving—even if you are still speaking with the adult.

Once you learn what the staff member wants, you will have a good idea of how much time it will take. If it requires a number of minutes, excuse yourself so that you can tell the student approximately when you will return. Your actions will let both parties know how much you value students and the way you respect all individuals.

Equally important is how to behave when students approach you while you are talking with someone else. Assume they have an important need, and briefly excuse yourself. Turn to the student, and, once you have ascertained the nature of the request, say how long you expect to be before you will be able to respond. (Remind students, if necessary, to say "excuse me" when they need to interrupt.)

Developing Respect

You are talking to a student and a teacher comes in to speak with you. What do you do?

_____

You are working with a student and your principal drops by. What do you do?

_____

Would you behave the same way if you were speaking with another adult when the interruption occurred?

_____

Did you use your philosophy in making your decision?

_____

LISTENING MATTERS

While the foregoing describes respectful ways of handling interruptions, being an active listener is another important skill for you to develop. You are always busy, and it is easy to rush to a solution with a student so that you can move on to the next task. Modes of language vary across the generations, and without being aware of it, you may misunderstand a request.

Take time to hear what is being said. Restate what you believe you heard and ask if that is what was meant. Be sure that your response was understood. Try hard not to be thinking of other things as you deal with the question. People—even young students—can sense impatience. Remind yourself that they are the reason for everything you do.

Somewhere in library school the "reference interview" was discussed. Asking students if a specific class prompted their request can help you identify what they need to find. Knowing whether they are searching for "youth in Asia" or "euthanasia" will save you and them from wasting time. Check to be sure that the answer you located or the source to which you directed someone met the information need.

Your listening will also serve as a role model for how you expect students to behave as well. In a world where instant messaging, blogging, cell phones, and text messaging are major forms of communication, young people are accustomed to getting their words out almost without paying any attention to what is coming in. It is a very egocentric environment. Yet one of the important skills students must master is learning to listen before jumping in with a question or comment. Even worse, they often fail to follow directions for an assignment, assuming they understand what was being asked without having really heard what was said.

Building listening skills begins at an early age. Preparing students for author visits, as discussed in chapter 6, is an opportunity to teach them how to tune in to what is being said so they won't repeat the same questions others have already inquired about. When you are teaching a class, you can further develop this ability by having them restate what you have said. (This will also help them learn to paraphrase.)

Listen Up

A high school student says he needs "books on Peru." What questions should you ask?

_____

_____

An elementary student makes the same request. What questions should you ask?

_____

_____

Did you ask if there was something specific about the country they needed to know?

_____

Did you check to find out if they needed maps or other graphics?

_____

A SENSE OF ORDER

While the "shushing" librarian (now a popular action figure) is still a prevailing stereotype, silent library media centers for the most part no longer exist, creating a problem for the new SLMS. How do you maintain discipline? How much noise is acceptable?

Dealing with Noise

You will need to find a tolerable noise level somewhere along the continuum, with absolute control at one end and chaos at the other. Both are unacceptable, but what is the ideal? The answer is not a matter of decibel level but rather a delicate balance of tolerance and flexibility. If it is impossible to hold a conversation because of the din, things are probably out of control. On the other hand, if you are in a large school and several classes are busy researching and students are also doing individual assignments, there will be lots of conversations going on. Most students are comfortable working and studying with a fair amount of background noise. Adults tend to prefer a quieter environment. You need to find an acceptable compromise—weighted toward what students prefer.

When a few students become gregarious and call across to friends, others raise their voices to speak over them and soon you are aware that the place is loud. Your knee-jerk reaction might lead you to shout out that everyone needs to get quieter. While this produces temporary results, avoid the practice except in those extreme cases when you cannot isolate the chief source of the noise. If you do this only rarely, students will recognize that they have pushed you too far.

Instead, to reduce the tumult, go over to the main culprits and remind them to lower their voices. On occasion, the leaders, looking for an opportunity to extend their fun, point out that they are not the only ones responsible. Calmly respond that you will attend to the others afterward but right now you are talking to them. Keep your word, and go over to the remaining noisy groups, bringing them the same message.

Another tactic students employ is to get you involved in a debate over their behavior. They will want to know what is too loud, or why the rule is necessary. Do not let them pull you off track. Avoid engaging in an argument and trying to out-reason them. You will be playing into their hands. Just calmly repeat that they need to lower their voices— and repeat it—and repeat it, until they realize they are not getting the reaction they want.

Flexibility comes into play at different times of the day or seasons of the year. If the LMC is filled during lunch period, you may allow a more sociable level of conversation. If you have a classroom or lab as part of the facility, you can make that a silent work area during this time for those who prefer quiet. Just before vacations, noise rises and you will drive yourself crazy if you try to maintain the usual decibel level. Just focus on keeping things from getting out of hand. The same advice holds in areas where snow can cause schools to close. If it appears that an early dismissal is possible, voices get louder—no matter what the students' ages are.

Approaches to Discipline

One of the trickiest aspects of discipline is what to do when teachers bring in their classes but ignore their students' behavior. Much like having invited a guest with unruly children into your home, you must be careful about what you do. If the disruption is limited, you can speak quietly to those causing the disturbance, reminding them of what is not appropriate in the LMC.

On occasion, teachers let their students get completely out of hand, and you need to be more assertive. Initially, ask them to get the class under control. Instead of making teachers feel wrong, suggest that students have become a bit too caught up in the assignment (or the impending vacation or whatever you can think of) and request that they be reminded to lower their voices. If teachers do not mind—or if it is a substitute who is in charge—you can take over. While it is still best to speak to individual tables, if you have delayed bringing order until the situation has really deteriorated, this is an occasion to raise your voice and let everyone know that the LMC has become far too loud.

New SLMSs (and teachers) tend to worry about discipline and look for prescriptions on how to maintain it. The real trick is not to think about discipline—just expect it. If you are concerned, students sense your uncertainty and tend to take advantage of it. Having built a climate of respect, you will find that they respond to the boundaries you set.

To Shush or Not to Shush

How do you personally feel about noise in the LMC?

_____

What might you say to a noisy table to keep the tone light and still get results?

_____

How would you let a teacher know that students are getting out of hand?

_____

GRADING

Ideally, SLMSs do not give grades. With all the pressures and labels placed on students, there should be one place where they do not feel judged. But for a number of reasons, sometimes you will have to give grades, and on occasion you might actively campaign for the right to do so.

Rigidly scheduled SLMSs have assigned classes and must do report cards—and even progress reports—to let parents and guardians know if their child is failing. It should be impossible for a student to fall into that category in the LMC. Think about what everyone should need to do to earn top grades and structure your requirements so that all students can meet them.

A common pitfall is to incorporate unacceptable behavior into the grade. While you want students to be mindful of how to act in the LMC, do not penalize them if they misbehave. Definitely do *not* take points off for failing to return books on time. Remind students of your expectations and tell them that you recognize that they know better. Grades, if you must give them, should be about knowing process skills, not conduct.

Assessing Students

How should you evaluate students' performance? Consider creating a rubric that you share with classes. Focus on the students' awareness of basic concepts and how to utilize these as part of the research process. Assess the students' willingness to explore rather than the specific results they find. You are the process, not the content, specialist.

Reward good questions whether they are asked during story time or as part of a skills lesson. Acknowledge the thinking process that went into them. Do not necessarily provide the answer. Throw it out to the class. Ask students where they could look for a solution. By showing you value questioning over rote repetition, you help develop inquiring minds, the first step in lifelong learning.

Welcome students' mistakes, showing them the opportunity to learn something new. Fearing to fail is an obstacle to intellectual growth. Help students discover the thinking process that caused their error and guide them into finding the right answer or an approach that solves the problem.

As you develop evaluation criteria, keep in mind as a fundamental principle that no one should ever fail "library." The LMC must be a place where students feel safe and successful. Receiving a bad grade will make them think they do not belong there.

Grading at the Secondary Level

At middle and high school levels, you will probably not be required to assign grades. However, you can raise your credibility by grading "works cited" pages. If you have done a lesson with a class as they start a research project, consider asking the teacher to let you review the sources students used. You would only be responsible for a fraction of the final mark, but students and teachers would benefit.

For example, students quickly recognize that if you are going to be grading a portion of their presentations, it would be wise to check with you for ideas on where to research, acquiring new skills as a result. With teachers, having someone knowledgeable overseeing the quality *and* credibility of sources used is often the beginning of a dialogue that leads to collaboration. While taking on this task will add to your workload, you get to see the impact of your teaching in the way students go about the assignment and you learn what changes you need to make in the future.

Meaningful Assessment

How can you use grades to promote your philosophy?

_____

Identify one skill that students should exhibit as they begin a research project.

_____

What different levels of expertise in that skill could be incorporated into a rubric?

_____

What would be a good question from a student?

_____

COCURRICULAR CONNECTIONS

New secondary teachers are expected to advise a club, sport, or other activity that is an intrinsic part of school life. Often you are not asked to take on this responsibility (which may or may not offer a stipend), but you should seriously consider doing so nonetheless.

As a class or student government adviser, you get to know the student leaders. While they are not the only ones who affect how you are viewed, they do influence a significant portion of the student body. Academic competition teams are another potential opportunity to use your expertise as you help them prepare for their meets.

Among the clubs, an anime group can be a resource for identifying graphic novels you should purchase, while an Internet group can work with you on a web page and provide you with student assistants. Consider any hobby or interest you have, whether it is scrapbooking or supporting environmental causes. See if there is a group and offer to assist the current adviser. Turnovers occur and you would then be the logical replacement.

Some cocurricular activities can conflict with the LMC schedule. You can rarely coach a sport because practice sessions are usually held every day after school during the season, making it impossible to keep the LMC open after hours. Other activities, such as mounting the school plays, are daunting, but if you enjoy them consider being one of the additional faculty helpers.

After you have been in your position for a year or two, you might even connect with students to start a new activity. One middle school SLMS decided to create a literary magazine. The reactions from students, teachers, and administrators enhanced her reputation and her program.

Whether or not you advise an activity, plan to attend some games or school plays. Students notice which faculty members show up. Watching students participate in something that is important to them reveals aspects of their personalities that you are not likely to see in the LMC environment. Be sure to praise the players or actors when you next see them. You will have added one more strand to the relationship you are weaving with students.

Broadening the Connection

What cocurricular activities appeal to you?

_____

Is there an area of such activities that you would like to develop with students?

_____

ONE-ON-ONE TEACHING

Numerous resources offer guidance in preparing lessons for classes at all grade levels, but do not overlook the importance of working with individuals. You are unique in the school in that you do both types of teaching—and that when you do help one person, it is not remediation.

Personal contact can take place at several levels. At the simplest, it comes in the form of a location request. "Where can I find . . . ?" Whether it is a book or information on the Web, always check back to see if students were successful in the search. Better yet, use an abbreviated reference interview to be sure you have understood their question. Sometimes the query is based on what they think is the place to look, but in actuality it is far off the mark.

Another variation occurs when you observe students at a computer clicking on one web page after another, or engaging in some other behavior that makes you realize they are having difficulty. Do not wait for a request for help. Some might never get to that step. Ask how they are doing and what they are trying to find. Offer a suggestion and see if they want more assistance. If they are content to go on by themselves, accept their decision. Not all students want you to work closely with them. When you have established a relationship and trust, they are more likely to be comfortable with letting you continue to help.

After a while, students will willingly seek your guidance as they do a research project. Use these individual instructional times to nurture the spirit of inquiry. Do not always tell them what to do next. Ask where they think they should look. If it is a blind alley, continue the questioning in a way that helps them recognize why that particular path did not bring results.

You might be challenged at first to decide how much help to give. The least amount of assistance is to guide students to the strategy they need (such as, "check the catalog"). The next level up is directing them to a specific location. Frequently you might accompany them to the stacks or work with them on the computer, and on occasion you get the information for them.

Over time you will learn what response best suits the situation. If the request is simple, let them try it on their own. When it seems that some instructional support is needed, you should work with them. However, when time is a factor, remember that you provide a service and don't have to teach every time. Occasionally you just need to help.

In all your dealings with students, you want to reveal to them how much they already know and how capable they are of getting to the next step. Showing off how much you know will not inspire them to learn more. A phrase to keep in mind is, "Be the guide on the side rather than the sage on the stage."

Working this way with students is rewarding to them as well as you. As no one else is there to hear it, they are less afraid of sounding stupid or foolish, and so they ask what they really need to know. They also enjoy being the center of your attention. The process allows you to focus on a specific need and ensure that students have grasped the concept. You get to see their thinking process and what assumptions you might have made about what they know or understand. For example, you might have said something about checking the domain on a website, and they don't know the term *domain*. This experience, particularly as you repeat it with other students, helps you to refine your strategies when you are teaching a class.

How you treat students during these one-on-one exchanges will affect what happens when you teach a large group in another way. Those who have gotten to know and respect you will pay more attention and focus on what you have to say. The more people in the class who feel that way, the easier the lesson will go.

Individual Attention

A student needs to use a book for a report on rain forests. What do you do?

_____

A student is having trouble finding a good website for a project. What do you do?

_____

Two students need a few books to bring back to class. What do you do?

_____

DEVELOPING LIFELONG LEARNERS

The various ideas presented in this chapter all serve to turn students into lifelong learners, but to fully achieve this goal you need to recognize what attitudes they must develop. Most education today focuses on the cognitive domain of Bloom's taxonomy. However, if you want to have an impact on students' learning behavior and attitudes outside of school, you must concentrate on the affective domain.[1]

Receiving, which includes awareness and selected attention, is the lowest level of the affective domain.[2] Similar to *knowledge* in the cognitive domain, it requires the least level of connection. Simply stated, it means that students focus on the lesson.

Responding requires a more active participation. Among the verbs associated with it are *ask, react, read,* and *respond.* These come into play when students seek help, which connects to the first indicator of the Information Literacy Standards—the information-literate student "recognizes the need for information."[3]

Once students reach *valuing,* which ranges from acceptance to commitment, they are beginning to develop the motivation necessary for lifelong learning. At this level they appreciate the worth of learning for its own sake. Although a number of verbs are possible, *choose* best illustrates this behavior. If students are encouraged to explore topics of interest to them, they want to find out more and come to value seeking information.

Organization refers to bringing together values that may be in conflict to build one's personal value system. Although verbs such as *defend, generalize,* and *group* are also used in the cognitive domain, here they are connected with intangibles. For lifelong learning to occur, students must want to have an ever-expanding knowledge base in order to be the person they wish to be.

The highest level of the affective domain, *characterization by a value or value complex,* sounds more complicated than it is. It simply means having internalized a set of values which becomes a lifestyle, in this case, that of lifelong learning. Verbs such as *exemplify, support,* and *uphold* illustrate this behavior.

Habits are not cognitive. They are based on what gives pleasure. If you want students to become lifelong learners, they must enjoy it. Much of what occurs in the school environment is apt to discourage learning. The LMC is the place where you can foster delight and satisfaction in knowing for its own sake. By making the LMC a safe place where students feel accepted for who they are, where they and their information needs are treated with respect, and where the SLMS models lifelong learning, you will achieve your goal.

Forming Habits

Which affective domains do you address during one-on-one instruction?

_____

How do you model being a lifelong learner?

_____

Key Ideas

- Smiles go a long way from the first day to the last.
- Learning students' names may be difficult but brings large results.
- Respect is the foundation of a good relationship.
- Treat students with the same courtesy that you use with adults.
- Active listening is a skill that both you and students need to master.
- Determine the most appropriate noise level for the LMC.
- Discipline is easy if you expect it and have built a climate of respect.
- Tread carefully when teachers fail to discipline their class in the LMC.
- Grading is sometimes necessary, but use it as an opportunity to encourage a spirit of inquiry.
- No one should fail in the LMC.
- Cocurricular assignments increase your credibility with students.
- Make time to attend school functions.
- Individual instruction can be the most important teaching you do.
- To develop lifelong learners, focus on the affective domain.
- Be a role model for lifelong learning.

NOTES

1. "Taxonomy of Educational Objectives," Humboldt State University, http://www.humboldt.edu/~tha1/bloomtax.html.
2. "Bloom's Taxonomy: Affective Domain," University of Mississippi, School of Education, http://www.olemiss.edu/depts/educ_school2/docs/stai_manual/manual9.htm.
3. American Association of School Librarians, Association for Educational Communications and Technology, *Information Power: Building Partnerships for Learning* (Chicago: American Library Association, 1998), 9.

CHAPTER 6

Reaching Your Teachers

Maybe the apples will help to bring the teachers in.

Core Ideas
- *Information Power*
- Your Philosophy
- Being a Teacher First

Building Trust and Relationships
- Teacher Care
- Confidentiality

Developing Collaboration
- Basics
- Baby Steps

Becoming a Partner
- Being an Instructional Partner
- Curriculum Mapping
- Sharing Trends
- Acquiring Leadership Skills

Teacher Styles
- Differentiated Planning
- "Challenging" Teachers

Author Visits
- Choosing an Author
- Planning
- Related Projects
- Preparing Questions
- Final Thoughts

*E*very aspect of your job is important, but none is as critical as your relationship with the teachers in your building. Your interaction with them has a direct bearing on the success of the school library media program. As noted in chapter 1, teachers are the gateway to your students. After the first days in a small school, you probably know most of the faculty by sight. If you are in a large building, there are some you may not meet during the entire year. However, it is now time to develop the connections with teachers that will define your program.

CORE IDEAS

As you settle into the school year, you need to touch base with concepts in *Information Power*, remind yourself of your philosophy, and determine the best way to start collaborating with teachers—even if you have a fixed schedule. Taking time for this reflection gives you the overview you need to stay focused and prevents you from feeling drowned in details.

Remember while you are working to reach teachers that you are also one yourself. You are part of the faculty. Never think of it as a "we-they" relationship. It is always "us." Teaching is the heart and soul of what you do, and not only with students. Every day, in ways both obvious and subtle, you coach teachers and others who come into the library media center.

Information Power

Reread pages 3–5 of *Information Power.* It states that you are expected to foster "the full range of information concepts, strategies, and abilities students must master" as well as those they need "to interact effectively with information and to construct meaningful knowledge." Then, in explaining how you are the "essential link" in the learning community, it identifies teaching as the first of your four roles (teacher, instructional partner, information specialist, and program administrator).[1]

The description of how you are to function within your building probably seems a far cry from reality. In many places, no one thinks of you as a "curricular leader and a full participant on the instructional team."[2] But instead of deciding that this concept is visionary rather than an achievable goal, start acting as though it were true. By behaving as a leader and always being prepared to participate (even if only informally), you will change how others perceive you. Ignoring what the national guidelines consider as your purpose will only lead to your minimizing it. How do you expect anyone else to view you as vital to the educational program if you don't see yourself that way?

Your Philosophy

Remember that your philosophy is what grounds you. Until it is a natural part of how you behave, you should look it over at least once a week. How does being student centered affect your interactions with teachers? You cannot be critical of them if they seem to put tests and benchmarks first, but you can make suggestions that tweak a planned unit so that it has greater flexibility and allows students more choices in their own learning.

Look for teachers who best model your philosophy in action. They are likely to be your first partners and may become your friends. Reserve judgment on those who seem diametrically opposite to your core values. As you become more familiar with them, you might discover that you caught them on an off day or that they are coping with a difficult mix of students. If you figure out why they take a particular approach, you can start with where they are and slowly win them over to your way of thinking.

Being a Teacher First

Your teaching ability is what will gain you the respect of the faculty. Without it, the best teachers will not happily trust you with their students. See if a mentor—official or not—can watch you in action. If that is not possible, review with that person a few of your lesson plans to get important feedback. Sometimes you may be able to videotape your presentation, which is almost as good as being observed.

Recognize that you will always be "on." It is easier for teachers who only have to look good for a day when parents come in to see their children's classes; you are always on view. If you have volunteers, you can be sure they are not just attending to their assigned tasks. They are watching and judging you. Teachers walk in during their free time, and while looking for something in the LMC, take note of how you are doing with a class.

You will be assessed by your colleagues in far more detail than by your principal or supervisor. The grapevine in a school is always active, so word will spread. If you think a lesson did not go well, let others know you recognize it before the word gets out. You can give a reason for why you were off, but also ask for advice from teachers (or even your supervisor) on how they might have handled a similar situation. When people help you, they have an investment in your success.

If you are open to learning, you can easily become a great teacher. When any of the really excellent ones are in the LMC, watch them at work. See how they are aware of all their students. What words of encouragement do they use? How do they make students feel valued? What do they do to get complex ideas across?

You can learn almost as much from less successful teachers. You might see how they shut down some students or make others angry and difficult to manage. Are they presenting too many concepts too fast? Do interactions feel stressful? What is causing the problem?

Think of the LMC as your teaching laboratory. Unbeknown to the teachers who come in, you see their best and worst practices in action. Each one can be a mini-lesson to add to the techniques you use to make your own teaching more effective.

Getting Grounded

What words in the early pages of *Information Power* do you find inspiring?

_____

Which part of your philosophy is most relevant to your work with teachers?

_____

Which teachers seem most likely to try a collaborative lesson with you?

_____

What are some great teaching practices you have observed?

_____

What are some bad ones?

_____

BUILDING TRUST AND RELATIONSHIPS

You will not have a dynamic SLMP overnight. While you want to keep your ultimate goals high, be realistic as to when they will be achieved. To fully implement all your ideas will take at least three to five years. You need to learn the curriculum, your collection, and the ins and outs of your school building and district. You will not know your students' strengths, weaknesses, and idiosyncrasies until you have worked with them. Reaching your entire faculty (in a small school) or a sizable percentage of them (in a large school) will require persistence and time.

Whether you are fresh out of library school and filled with the confidence of knowing what constitutes a good program or you are coming from one you developed in another school, you will not win support by telling people how they need to change. If you talk too much about what is wrong, you will be ignored or worse. Some more experienced teachers are likely to disregard anyone obviously new to the profession as idealistic and not very practical. Their attitude is that they know best; they have been doing their job for years. They can be equally dismissive if you talk about your previous district and will see it as not applicable to their situation, or possibly become resentful because they feel you are belittling their school. Think before you speak. You don't want to spend precious time making amends for remarks someone found offensive or irritating.

Teacher Care

Since nurturing relationships with teachers is fundamental to your success (although it is not one of the many items listed in your job description), you must always look for ways to reach them. The teacher area recommended in chapter 4 is one idea. Having photocopiers in the LMC is another. As teachers need to get copies made, they become frequent visitors.

When teachers drop by, engage them in conversation whenever possible. Rather than bringing up collaboration ideas, focus on who they are as people and what is important in their lives. If you talk about the job before you have built a relationship, they will dread coming in. However, they will love to have a welcoming ear to share their problems and their joys. As you get to know each other better, it will be easier and more natural to also discuss a possible project.

Having food available is another lure. Teachers often are busy and skip lunch. If they get hungry and know you always have something to munch on, they will drop by. Sometimes they miss breakfast and appreciate being able to grab a snack in the LMC. The rules for conversation here are the same as with the copiers: *first* the relationship, then the job. Many of your regulars will eventually contribute to the goodies, making them feel they are part of the LMC—an attitude you definitely want to cultivate.

While you should not use scarce budget dollars to buy recreational reading for teachers, you can offer them acquisitions you think will interest them. This is relatively simple at a high school, where you purchase many adult books. Once you get to know their preferences, you can let them borrow a new title even before it is shelved. Be careful, because some teachers may keep it for most of the year. Let them have only one until you see how quickly it is returned. (If necessary, remind them that you have other people waiting for that book.)

At the elementary level—as well as middle and high school—show your regulars books they might want to use with their classes. Whether it is a new picture book or a reference work, they will appreciate your thinking of them. If they appear to really like one of the titles you can suggest a possible project with it.

Confidentiality

Showing teachers that you respect them and going the extra step to help is important in developing the relationships that are crucial to future collaboration. Some of this was probably discussed in library school. What you do not hear about is the value of learning to be trustworthy.

Trust is at the heart of relationships. Without it, you hold a piece of yourself in reserve. If you want to work well with teachers, you must earn their trust. They need to feel safe when speaking with you. As noted earlier, the grapevine in schools is not only alive and well—it is very fast. You want to avoid contributing to it, particularly when you have heard some juicy bit of gossip or personal information.

Teachers need opportunities to vent. They often come to the LMC and explode about other teachers, administrators, parents, or students. It may be an ongoing issue or a one-day crisis. Whatever it is, say the appropriately soothing words, such as "that had to be very upsetting" or "I can see it really made you angry." Provide no ammunition for the teacher to take away, and *never* repeat what was said.

By not spreading what was told to you in confidence, you build trust. Teachers having a bad day will feel safe in coming to you. They will eventually tell you of troubles at home as well as on the job. While *you* should not complain about school matters (keep those for conversations with SLMSs outside the district), you can talk about your personal issues. Through these honest exchanges, you will get to know and trust each other. The relationship will grow and collaboration will follow.

Getting to Know You

What do you ultimately want to achieve in your relations with teachers?

_____

What can you realistically accomplish with them the first year?

_____

What strategies will you use to build those relationships?

_____

With whom can you safely talk about frustrations and problems you may encounter on the job?

_____

DEVELOPING COLLABORATION

Although you were drilled in library school on the importance of collaboration with teachers, you may not have learned how to begin. If you are rigidly scheduled, teachers seem to want you only for the preparation period you give them. Even in schools where classes are scheduled as needed, teachers may be looking for the room and possibly the resources, but not you.

Full collaboration, where you are equal partners in presenting a unit, takes time to develop. Do not see teachers' reluctance to work with you as a failure on their part. Look at it from their perspective.

Basics

Teachers have no reason to change. As far as they can tell, they have been doing fine without you. They are concerned about high-stakes tests, standards, adequate yearly progress, and curriculum timelines. The pressures on them are intense. They see collaborating with you as keeping them from what they have to get done, and it sounds like a lot more work. And they are right.

But of course, they *do* have a reason to change. You know collaboration brings better results. You really want to tell them how great it will be if only you can work together. Realize that convincing them is like trying to describe a sunset to someone who is color-blind. Those who have not seen this partnership in action have no idea of why they would want it.

Do not let your frustration show. Complaints will only keep teachers away from you. So, how can you move them from disinterested colleagues to active partners?

You must be the one to reach out. Do not wait for teachers to come to you, and do not expect to succeed with your first suggestion. Keep the dialogue going. If one idea is ignored, wait a while and try another.

Baby Steps

Your first project should not be elaborate. For example, if a class comes to the LMC to do research and you were not asked to give any instruction, observe what they are doing. Select something in your collection that would be *most* helpful. Perhaps it is one of your electronic databases or a new reference set.

Once students have begun their research, show the teacher what you have. Offer to introduce it to the class—taking no more than ten minutes. Not only is this usually acceptable, but sometimes what you present becomes a requirement. As the period draws to a close, mention that you would be more than happy to do this with the next project. If once again you are not asked for help, repeat the process without showing any annoyance. Eventually, the teacher will talk to you about a research assignment before bringing the class to the LMC.

If you are rigidly scheduled, you will need to be even more creative. Listen carefully at lunch to learn what teachers are planning. Come up with a simple project students can finish in no more than two sessions in the LMC. Check to be sure that it will complement and not conflict or overlap with what is being done in the classroom. Have students do something large for their final product. Make an accompanying sign identifying the class and teacher when you display it in the LMC.

When the activity is completed, invite the teacher in to see it. Suggest that you would love to do more of this. Offer to write it up for the school newsletter going to parents. Depending on the relationship you managed to build so far, you may be asked to do another one. If not, continue to listen for ideas at lunch.

Collaboration implies joint responsibility beginning with the planning stage, but you will not reach that for a while. Because teachers are justifiably hesitant to add to their load, at first you must do most of the work. Once they see the results, find that information literacy skills spill over into higher-order thinking skills in the classroom, and recognize your abilities as a teacher, they will become increasingly interested in working with you.

Teaching Almost Together

What lesson have you done either in library school, your field experience, or in a previous school that might lend itself to your new situation?

_____

What is your best resource for a social studies class? Language arts? Science?

_____

Which teachers will you reach out to first?

_____

BECOMING A PARTNER

While collaboration is a partnership, it only lasts as long as the assignment. Being an "instructional partner" as defined in *Information Power* is an ongoing role.[3] Once you have reached that level, working with teachers on projects occurs more frequently and naturally.

Being an Instructional Partner

To be able to take a "leading role in developing policies, practices, and curricula that guide students to develop the full range of information and communication abilities," you must serve on committees or teams that affect these areas.[4] Learn which are the powerful ones in your district or school and try to get on them.

For example, there may be a curriculum committee with significant input on courses that will be added or dropped. Knowing changes ahead of time helps you plan effectively. More important, you can then work with the teachers who are designing the new programs and become an integral part of them.

Some districts are developing "professional learning communities." These not only affect what and how subjects are taught but also form important relationships. Whether or not you are compensated for the extra time, it is worth your effort to join one, since in exchange you get a forum for showing the value of a strong SLMP.

High schools (and some lower schools as well) go through an accreditation process. While everyone usually serves on at least one committee, you want to be part of a major one, such as steering. You will be working with the strongest teachers in the building, which will add to your own understanding of how the school works. Additionally, you will have an opportunity to let them get to know you better, and, to some extent, promote the SLMP.

If your district does site-based management, you must find a way to be on the core team. Of course, as with the accrediting process, you will be getting familiar with the more powerful teachers. More critically, you will help determine the allocation of budget dollars. SLMSs who are not part of this process frequently find they have little or no funds.

Curriculum Mapping

Many districts are doing curriculum mapping to prevent overlap of instruction and to stay focused on goals and standards. The process involves collecting information about what is taught and keying it to the school calendar. For example, the final document may show that the third grade studies several biomes in February and will give the objectives, resources, standards, and assessments for that unit. This helps teachers to understand when students learned what and where they are going next.

Curriculum mapping is usually subject-related, so teachers (and administrators) may not understand at first why you should be a member of the committee. Explain that as the information specialist you can be of help in locating information outside the district. Once the team turns to what is to be taught and when, your role will be to identify the existing resources that complement the units.

The benefits to your SLMP can be enormous. First, as with any important committee, you get to be among the building leaders, letting them see that you bring an added dimension to the educational community. Next, you become familiar with what is being taught at each grade level or subject area and when these units occur. This knowledge is a tremendous help in making purchasing decisions.

Last, serving on this committee puts you in a great position to build collaboration. Knowing which topics would benefit from research, you can plug them in. Teachers who would have never considered working with you now see these projects in the curriculum map. While they may be hesitant, you are aware of what the objectives are and have the needed resources. You will be able to guide the process, easing teacher stress, and will integrate "the information and communication abilities required to meet subject matter standards."[5]

Some of the best materials on curriculum mapping are available through the Association for Supervision and Curriculum Development (ASCD). If your LMC does not have books on the topic, go to the ASCD website (http://www.ascd.org) and purchase a few. Become familiar with the process, and then volunteer for any committees dealing with it.

Sharing Trends

One of your responsibilities is to keep current with what is new in technology and the library profession. Going to state or national library conferences is the easiest way to stay up-to-date. Even if your district doesn't reimburse you, you should do all in your power to attend. In some cases this may mean taking personal days, but it is important for your professional development and for becoming a partner with your teachers.

When you return from these conferences, you are filled with enthusiasm and new ideas you want to try. Talk to those teachers who want to be in the forefront of technology or to try new classroom approaches. Even if you do not follow up with a unit together, you will be demonstrating that you know what is happening in education today and therefore are a good resource.

Reading professional journals will also keep you abreast of what is happening. However, you already have a huge job with an enormous workload. Although this is not a high priority, find some time to review key journals and scan their articles. Focus first on those journals relating to libraries. *School Library Journal* (which you also read for book reviews) is a major one. The authors' own publication, *The School Librarian's Workshop,* a 24-page bimonthly newsletter for K–12 SLMSs, is another source (http://www.school-librarians-workshop.com). In addition to dealing with LMC specifics, it also covers what is going on in education in general.

For a broader view, look at periodicals such as *Educational Leadership,* published by the ASCD, *Phi Delta Kappan* (which has wonderful educational cartoons), and *Instructor.* There are some shortcuts that will help speed the process. *Educational Leadership* has a theme in each issue, so you can put aside those that do not seem to have a major impact on what is happening in your school. In looking at these journals, focus on articles that are about the grade levels in your building. Scan opening and closing paragraphs, check tables and other supporting items, and look for new terminology. Think of how you could use the information— and with what teachers. This will help fix concepts in your mind. Then discuss it with the faculty members you have identified.

For subject-related journals such as *English Journal,* check the table of contents to see if anything would be of interest to particular teachers. Put notes in their boxes to let them know you are holding it for them.

When possible, be sure to chat about the article either when they check the magazine out or, better yet, when they return it.

Once you realize that it will not take you forever to get through all the material, you will be more likely to flip through the journals. As you pick up new ideas and become familiar with trends in education, you can share them informally with teachers. Your awareness of what is happening—and what soon might affect their jobs—makes them recognize you as a valuable, and nonjudgmental, resource. When their supervisors ask them to incorporate a new approach and they are uncertain how to do it, they will turn to you. Most often, you can best help them by demonstrating the technique in a collaborative project.

Acquiring Leadership Skills

Although this section has been exploring how you become a "partner," what underlies it is learning how to become a leader. Leading is relatively easy when you have a job that implies authority. Teachers respond to principals not necessarily because of their leadership skills but because of their title.

No one will ask you to take on a leadership role. You will not be given any authority. So how do you emerge as a building leader and why is it important?

There are several answers to the last question. On the most basic level, it is a matter of survival. The jobs of those recognized as leaders are rarely eliminated. School library media specialists perceived that way are less likely to have their staff cut, and their budgets are reduced only when there are no other options. Because you have become a presence in the building, teachers are more willing to collaborate with you, since they get recognition from you and their supervisors for doing so. Your program thrives, and students benefit.

Knowing that it is important, how do you become a leader? If you have been following suggestions from this and previous chapters, you are already on your way. You need to have a compelling vision for where you want to go, be willing to take risks (small ones until you become established), accept responsibility, stay current with technology and educational trends, and be able to work well with everyone by discovering and acknowledging their individual strengths.

What you cannot do is hide in the LMC, expecting that people will notice what you do. You will never emerge as a leader if you complain about your workload, assume that what you learned in library school is enough to keep you up-to-date for a few years, and do not volunteer for committees or to be an adviser to cocurricular activities. Leadership is positive and proactive.

Although becoming a leader sounds daunting, just focus on what you want to achieve and accept setbacks as bumps on the road. You will increasingly gain the respect of teachers and others. Before long you will be regarded as a leader.

Partners in Education

On what committees would you now want to serve?

_____

What are the dates for your state's next library conference? How do you plan to get permission to attend?

_____

To which professional journals does the LMC subscribe?

_____

What do you think is your greatest leadership strength? Weakness?

_____

TEACHER STYLES

You are aware that students learn differently and have probably incorporated Howard Gardner's multiple intelligences into lesson plans.[6] Teachers also have their individual learning styles and personality traits. You need to be conscious of what works best with each of them if you are going to be successful in collaborating with them.

Some teachers prefer a written exchange—e-mail and attachments—to outline what will be covered, who will do what, and what the culminating project will be. Others want to touch and look at the resources you plan to use without you hovering over them. A few like to have several in-depth discussions with you. And then there are those who still want to just show up and assume the students will figure out how to get the task done.

Differentiated Planning

Some teachers will never want to work with you. While you can sometimes win them over, expend your energy in working with those who do. As you become increasingly familiar with teachers, you can use Anthony F. Gregorc's Mind Styles Model, which offers a Gregorc Style Delineator to begin mentally categorizing them into those who are concrete sequential (CS), abstract sequential (AS), concrete random (CR), and abstract random (AR).[7] Each of these personality types will require a different approach from you.

CS teachers are highly focused and do not want side chatter. Those who are AS are big-picture people who want to see the overall design before getting down to details, although they are anchored in academics. The CRs like to try something new, while the ARs love something that is touchy-feely. All types need you to bring a bit of balance in a way they can accept.

Most CS people tend to have rigid requirements for students and want a limited amount of time in the LMC. Try brief projects, but look to build in a variety of final products to allow students some personal choices. Be sure that they have to complete similar steps or components.

AS teachers come in with a large topic. They may want to give students free rein in choosing something within it, but they still want a traditional paper. Indicate, although you need not spell out the details, that you will be helping the students develop strategies to find their specific topics. Explore the possibilities of having a group project in addition to the written report.

CRs are fun because they want to be on the cutting edge. Since they look for something different each year, you want to start by brainstorming possibilities. If you have a new database, you can probably integrate it into the students' research. Be sure to discuss trends you have identified in your professional reading and see how many of them can be woven in as well.

Reining in the ARs can present a challenge. They are willing to spend a number of periods in the LMC, but sometimes it seems as though they will let students take endless time in search of a direction. They usually have the class work in groups and do not always notice or care that they are socializing far more than researching. Suggest ways for individual accountability within the group's overall responsibility.

"Challenging" Teachers

In any school, some teachers present a challenge. They may come to the LMC, but every encounter with them seems fraught with problems. Although they fall into the four personality types described above, they manifest these traits in ways that get your back up. You almost wish they would never come in. Understanding what these teachers need to feel secure is the key to dealing with them.

Controlling teachers need security. They are uncomfortable in the open, relaxed atmosphere of the LMC. Suggest that each day's work have a task that can be graded. Students can complete work sheets and maintain logs of their activities.

Some "stars" do not like the "shared billing" of a collaborative project. Propose large culminating activities that can be put on display with their names alongside the projects. For your first endeavors, these can be hung in the corridors rather than in the LMC. Acknowledge these teachers as the content experts. Your role is to help students with the process.

For teachers who always have a somewhat reserved, professional demeanor, you want to make a point of the standards that will be addressed. Be sure to acquaint them with the National Educational Technology Standards for Students.[8] These teachers will appreciate covering a new but required aspect of learning. Create a well-crafted lesson plan and show it to them in advance. Ask for their input, and take their advice.

A few teachers are so laid-back that their classes are noisy, unfocused, and regard the periods in the LMC as play time. Go along with the open-ended assignment and allow students to begin in the loose way they expect. After ten minutes, call everyone together and have a focusing discussion on what is working and what is not. The good thing is that these teachers do not take it personally if you remind the class about appropriate behavior.

Making It Personal

What are some personality types you can identify in the teachers you have begun to know?

_____

How would you describe your personality type? Is it similar to or different from the teachers you like best?

_____

Which teachers seem to present a challenge? Are their personality types similar? What does that suggest to you?

_____

AUTHOR VISITS

Discussing author visits may seem odd in a chapter devoted to reaching teachers, but these visits have a far greater impact if you involve the faculty. You will want to select the author with care, prepare students (and teachers) in advance, thoroughly plan for the event (making sure your guest is well-treated), and have an activity that connects to the day of the visit.

Choosing an Author

Your favorite authors or illustrators may not be the best persons to invite. Not all authors are good speakers or are comfortable with students at the age level for which they will be presenting. Never make arrangements without first carefully checking around. Listening to authors at a conference is one way to learn if they will be appropriate for your students. Contact other SLMSs who have had guests for their recommendations. Your state library association's electronic discussion list is another place to request information. Ask for suggestions, and be sure you have specified the grade levels with which you work.

Authors are not free, so you will also need to find out if the ones you want are in your price range. Unless an author's program is already in place in your school, you probably will not be able to set this up in your first year, but you can begin the preliminary work. Check to see where you can get funding. The usual sources are parent-teacher associations or local educational foundations.

Find out what the authors are willing to do. How many talks will they give and for how long? Do they present only lectures or do they engage in discussions with students? What is the largest size group they will address? Is there a limit to the amount of autographing they will do?

Planning

Preparing students and teachers is the key to the success of the author's visit. You will need to let everyone know who is coming and when. In a high school, you will deal with only a few teachers in one or two departments. Keep the supervisors informed and be sure to invite them to the presentations. Check that students are familiar with the author's works. For primary grades, you or the teachers can read the author's books throughout the year, calling attention to particular themes or, in the case of illustrators, to artistic techniques. With upper grades, maintain a display of the author's titles, and be sure to purchase additional copies so there will be enough for students to borrow.

If you start at the beginning of the school year to prepare students and teachers for your guest's visit by publicizing the date and the author's website, having them read and become familiar with titles and think about questions they would like to ask, the day should be very successful. Authors appreciate coming to schools where students already know their work and can make intelligent comments and ask perceptive questions.

Order books to sell for autographing well in advance. Invite parents to attend if there is space. Ask for parent volunteers for the day, since you will need as many extra hands as you can get.

Related Projects

Talk with teachers and look for curricular connections to the author's writings. In addition, devise some projects that connect with the author's work. These should be completed shortly before the visit so they can be shared with your guest and others who attend. Depending on whom you have invited, there are many possibilities for connections. The following are a few examples.

A "magic tree house" was built in the library media center in honor of a visit by Mary Pope Osborne. Every student received a half sheet of paper and was asked to use one side to make an illustration for the author, while on the other side they wrote a question, made a comment, or suggested a title or plot for an upcoming book. These were attached like shingles all around the tree house, giving students the opportunity for one-to-one contact with the author, who took all the pages home with her at day's end.

Collaboration between a second grade teacher, an art teacher, and the SLMS produced a project when poet Douglas Florian came to speak. Students selected an insect, researched it, and then, using their notes, wrote a poem about their choice. They then worked on a painting of their subject in art class. The poems, done on the computer in different type styles, were arranged around their paintings and pasted together in a striking manner in a booklet entitled *Insects and More.* The poet was deeply impressed, commenting to each child, and was the center of a class picture.

When author-illustrator David Wisniewski was the guest, first grade students, enthralled by his stories and his cut-paper illustrations, done using X-acto blades, brainstormed a tale of their own and prepared an exciting big book called *Space Players* complete with cut-paper illustrations (using scissors instead), which he was delighted to accept as a gift.

A second grade teacher and the SLMS designed an unusual and exciting alphabet book in honor of author-illustrator Jose Aruego's visit. Since he generally illustrated animals in his picture books, theirs was entitled *Aruego's Zoo,* and each student was responsible for researching an animal for one letter. They learned a lot and enjoyed the project immensely, as did Aruego when he was given the finished product.

Preparing Questions

You should help students both understand and review the kinds of questions they might want to ask the author, adding still another dimension to the visit. Many students will be interested in the same information: how long the person has been writing or illustrating, how many books have been produced, which one is the author's favorite, facts about the family. They must listen carefully to the entire presentation, because often these popular questions are answered within it. Students shouldn't be so busy concentrating on when they will be able to ask *their* questions that they miss hearing what they wanted to know. Moreover, the presenter may surmise that they have not been listening or paying attention to what was being said.

Students must also be alert and focus on the dialogues between their classmates and the guest as others ask questions, so they do not repeat any. With practice, they will discover the value of listening, will absorb much more information, and their questions will become better.

Final Thoughts

Give your guest precise directions to the school and the start and end time for the day, as well as your phone number both at home and at school in case a problem arises. While you may have a number of people joining you at lunch, be sure there is adequate time for the author to eat and relax. Have bottled water readily available throughout the day. Make sure the check is ready for your guest before the day ends.

Finally, write letters promptly to everyone who helped make the day a success—the funding source, parents who served lunch or oversaw the autographing, and especially the guest, mentioning good comments by teachers, students, and parents. If your author has enjoyed the day, he or she will often put in a good word for your school with a popular colleague who may become your next year's celebrity.

Author, Author

Is there a program for author visits in your school? Who is responsible for it?

_____

Where would you go to get funding for one?

_____

List three reasons why having an author visit would benefit students.

_____

_____

_____

Key Ideas

- ◼ You must have good relations with teachers to have a successful program.
- ◼ Learn best practices from both good and bad teachers.
- ◼ Focus on your vision while keeping your expectations to a minimum.
- ◼ Don't criticize your new school or any members of the staff.
- ◼ Work on creating relationships before you push for collaboration.
- ◼ Recognize the stresses in teachers' lives.
- ◼ Continue to suggest new ideas.
- ◼ Don't repeat gossip or confidences.
- ◼ Start with small cooperative projects.
- ◼ Volunteer for important committees.
- ◼ By being involved with curriculum mapping, you can integrate the SLMP into all subject areas.
- ◼ Read professional journals and share what you learn with teachers.
- ◼ Becoming a building leader is vital to the success of your program.
- ◼ Differentiate the planning process in order to respond to teacher personalities.
- ◼ In dealing with teachers, one size does not fit all. You must vary your approach.
- ◼ Even difficult teachers can be managed if you understand their needs.
- ◼ Author visits are another vehicle for working with teachers.
- ◼ Make curricular connections to enrich the value of author visits.

NOTES

1. American Association of School Librarians, Association for Educational Communications and Technology, *Information Power: Building Partnerships for Learning* (Chicago: American Library Association, 1998), 3–5.
2. Ibid., 4.
3. Ibid., 4–5.
4. Ibid.
5. Ibid., 5.
6. Howard Gardner, *Frames of Mind: The Theory of Multiple Intelligences* (New York: Basic Books, 1993).
7. Anthony F. Gregorc, *Gregorc Style Delineator: Development, Technical, and Administration Manual* (New York: Gabriel Systems, 1984). See also "Gregorc Associates Inc.," http://www.gregorc.com.
8. "Technology Foundation Standards for All Students," National Educational Technology Standards for Students, http://cnets.iste.org/students/s_stands.html.

CHAPTER 7

A Matter of Principals

With a little support, the library media program can really take off.

First Steps
- Who Is in Charge?
- *Information Power*

Informal Communication
- Unscheduled Visits
- Chats
- E-Mail

Formal Communication
- Reports
- Memos
- Meetings

Dos and Don'ts
- Choosing Your Format
- Bringing Bad News

Observations and Evaluations

Building Support
- Being Supportive
- Sharing Common Perspectives

*A*lthough contacts with your principal or supervisor are likely to be far less frequent than with teachers, every meeting is important. Since they occur more rarely, these encounters are all significant, each adding something to her overall impression of you and the school library media program. Whether or not the two of you are discussing it, your constant subtext is to build support for the SLMP. How well you handle communications with your administrator can have a significant effect on your success.

FIRST STEPS

Unless there is something critical, take time to get to know students and teachers before reaching out to your principal. You want to feel comfortable in your new position first. Of course, if she wants to see you, the initial chat cannot be delayed. Listen carefully and be as upbeat as you can, keeping options open for further talks.

Use this time to develop a sense of how the principal is viewed by the faculty. Does she stand by teachers or cave in to parental pressures? Try to figure out her style. Is she to the point or does she prefer a more informal, touchy-feely approach? Think of Gregorc's Mind Styles Model which you used for teachers.[1] Having a sense of how the principal operates will help when you finally do get together.

Who Is in Charge?

When you are new and everything is unfamiliar, there is a tendency to ask your administrator for help. Seeking advice can be a positive, but this early in the game it will make you appear uncertain. Principals want their buildings to run smoothly. If they suspect you are being tentative, they will take over.

A principal once said, "Who is going to be the expert here—you or me?" The answer should be obvious. So what do you do when you are unsure? Depending on the issue, check with the other school library media specialists in your district or with an experienced mentor. (Some states have a formal program for this; in other places you will need to find a successful SLMS who is willing to help you out. Check with your library association for possible candidates.)

At the same time, be careful not to be dogmatic in your approach to your job. Try not to make any major decisions too early. Having a plan of action does not mean you must implement it immediately, although you can mention—in passing—to your principal that you have some ideas about where you want to take the SLMP. While these thoughts are open for discussion, you will be regarded as managing the library media center by being the one to bring them to the table.

Information Power

Connecting to national guidelines is a good technique for demonstrating your expertise and is an excellent opening for an early discussion with your principal. Although you need to be familiar with *Information Power* in its entirety, the ALA has a brochure with the nine Information Literacy Standards and what these have to offer to administrators, teachers, and students. You can get a package of twenty-five brochures for eight dollars (less if you are a member) at the ALA's online store (http://www.alastore.ala.org).

Give a copy of the brochure to your principal once the school year is under way, asking to discuss it at a later date. You may not get a response, so bring another copy with you whenever you have your first or second meeting with her. Keep the remaining brochures handy to give readily to other building administrators, interested teachers, or parents.

Become familiar with the language of *Information Power* so that you can use it easily when speaking with administrators. You want to know, understand, and communicate your four roles.[2] Up to this point, you have been stressing the first three (teacher, instructional partner, and information specialist) in your overtures to students and teachers. With your principal, you need to include the fourth—program administrator. Not only does this enhance your standing as an expert, but it also shows why you are a valuable member of a formal or informal leadership team.

Starting Right

What are your impressions of your principal? Your supervisor, if you have one?

_____

What one idea about the SLMP do you want her to know?

_____

How comfortable are you with your role as a program administrator?

_____

INFORMAL COMMUNICATION

Since almost every encounter with your principal has the potential for increasing or decreasing her regard for the SLMP and how well you manage it, all your communication with her is important. The size of the school and the relationship you develop with the principal will contribute to which format you use most frequently, but, particularly in the early days, think before you speak or write.

If the staff is small, you will probably speak informally with your principal frequently. Some administrators are at the sign-in desk in the office most mornings to greet teachers. A smile, a cheery hello, and a comment about the weather or a recent school event is sufficient. Do not try to seize the moment to bring up something important. This is not the time for a deep discussion.

Good administrators are always aware of what is happening in their building, including who arrives early and stays late. While you are never penalized for not extending your work hours, you do earn extra points by coming in ahead of the required time. It means you are among the faculty members who can be counted on to provide additional supervision in case of emergencies, as well as daily oversight in those buildings where students can enter as soon as doors are open. In the latter case this means that you make the LMC available to them so they can quietly socialize as well as complete homework.

Unscheduled Visits

One level up from greetings exchanged in the morning or when passing each other in the halls is an informal chat which might occur in the LMC or the principal's office. In the former instance, your administrator might pop into your room just to see how things are going. If you are in the middle of a class, acknowledge her presence with a nod of your head; otherwise walk over, welcome her, and ask what you can do for her. Particularly in the early stages of building your relationship, do not initiate requests and definitely do not make any complaints at this time. Just respond to what she wants.

On occasion, your principal may show up with visitors she is taking around the school. The LMC is a favorite stop. As in the first situation, do not interrupt what you are doing with a class. Allow your administrator to make any explanations—correct or not. If you do have a free moment, you can greet them and *briefly* explain why things are calm at this time. Unless you are engaged by your principal or the guests in further discussion, excuse yourself and get back to work.

It may seem to you that nothing has happened during these encounters, but in reality you have sent some important messages. Your principal now knows you have an understanding of what is appropriate, and, more important, that you will not be cornering her at every opportunity to criticize or ask for something. You have also shown that you can create a welcoming environment in the LMC for administrators as well as students and teachers.

Chats

When the informal encounter is in the principal's office, the content and nature of the conversation can be more substantive. This can be initiated either by you or the administrator. If you are the one making the request, it might be to bring a new service to her attention or to extend an invitation to a special event. While you can do this by e-mail, sometimes a face-to-face conversation has a greater impact and is more likely to produce results.

If you are lucky, you might catch your principal at the right time and see if she has a few minutes to speak with you, or ask the secretary to schedule you for ten minutes. The key is to be brief and to the point. Do not go beyond your allotted time. If you happen to get your "mini-meeting" immediately, you should have all the information with you. Succinctly provide any necessary background. For example, is the service a replacement of an existing one, an extension of what is already available, or totally brand new? How will it improve student achievement? (That is always a critical aspect.) When you want your administrator to attend an event, be sure to specify who will be there and why her presence is important.

Never use these informal chats for a major discussion. For the most part, these chats are conducted on the fly. You might send a reminder e-mail, but the issues involved should be relatively easy to address. Save anything heavy-duty for a more formal venue.

Your principal may also initiate one of these chats, perhaps at the end of the day as you are signing out. You might be asked if you have a moment to talk. Unless you have an appointment and must leave (and in that situation, immediately suggest an alternate time to meet), graciously agree.

Do not anticipate the subject of the conversation. It may just be an attempt to get to know you better and see how you are doing. Keep your answers positive. If something is really bothering you, do not bring it up now. You are not prepared and are likely to make some missteps. Instead, say that you are putting together some ideas concerning whatever it is, and once that is done you will ask for a meeting about it. When you do request it, your principal, having remembered this brief mention, will be more open to listen.

While a good administrator will not use this informal approach to bring up concerns she may have about you, some will use this ploy, thinking that it will either keep you from getting too nervous or that it can be handled more quickly this way. Although you are upset and worried, stay calm. Do not be defensive. When you focus on trying to explain away the criticism, you are usually not listening to what is being said.

Concentrate on what is at the core of the problem. If you are not clear about it, have your principal explain what she wants you to do. Unless it is contrary to your philosophy, agree to follow her recommendations and suggest that you have a meeting in a few weeks to see how you are implementing them. By being the one to ask for the follow-up, you have taken charge of the situation, shown you are not threatened by criticism, and are open and willing to learn.

E-Mail

Even schools that do not permit access to personal accounts tend to use e-mail heavily within the district. Although e-mail is written, the attitude toward it is that it is an informal means of communication. It allows you to reach someone more easily than by phone and to send a more complex message than you would leave in voice mail—and therein lies the danger.

While it is always a good idea to reread an e-mail before sending it off, you should make it a habit to do so when in school. Spelling and grammatical idiosyncrasies that have become second nature since instant messaging are not usually acceptable in the academic setting. Since you cannot use emoticons, you want to make sure that what you are saying cannot be misconstrued by an alternate reading.

Who is or is not copied can be another minefield. Copying someone can sound like tattling, while not sending the e-mail to a key player might be construed as insulting. In general, try to avoid incurring complaints. A good example of how to use e-mail is informing a supervisor (and copying the principal) when a teacher has had a particularly successful project in the LMC. Another is to review key items from a meeting or to request such a review. In that case, you would copy all participants.

By now everyone should know that e-mail in the business setting is not private. Whatever you send can be retrieved. Make sure that you never say anything that you would not want announced in public.

Easy Does It

What is your principal's preferred method of informal communication?

_____

At what time of day and in what location is your principal most visible?

_____

What would be your response to a criticism of how you handled a student?

_____

What are some possible "light" topics for a chat with your principal?

_____

FORMAL COMMUNICATION

You will have regular opportunities to communicate formally with administrators. Sometimes these are required; in other cases you will initiate them. Although these exchanges may seem more significant than informal ones, recognize that not everything you send will be read completely or, in some instances, even skimmed. Nevertheless, you should treat each of them as one more step in encouraging support for your program.

Whether writing a memo or a report, take advantage of the format to reread and reflect upon what you have written. Obviously you should check for spelling and grammatical errors, but you should also make sure that you have expressed yourself clearly, avoided library jargon, and did not ramble. If you have another person working with you in the LMC, see if she will proofread and critique the document. Be open to suggestions. You know what you want to say, but if your reader does not get it, changes must be made.

If e-mail is the preferred means of communication in your building, send reports and memos as attachments. This will add the necessary formality, and you are more likely to have an impeccable document than if you simply put the information in the body of the e-mail. Administrators who prefer to hear from you electronically tend to read whatever they receive that way and are inclined to be more casual with hard-copy information.

Reports

Even if your principal does not expect them, you should prepare monthly reports that provide an overall record of what transpires in the LMC. Before you write your first one, review any that you found (see chapter 4) when organizing your office. Do they give you a sense of the SLMP? Do they give numbers for anything beyond circulation statistics?

Where reports are required, it is possible that the format is also stipulated. Check with your administrator to find out. Maintaining the existing pattern in your reports for a while is a good idea in any case. You have a guide as to what to include, and your principal has become accustomed to it. If you feel that the format does not give you room to adequately present the SLMP, you might ask whether you can make adaptations.

Reports should contain a balance between narrative and statistical information. In a high school and other flexibly scheduled LMCs, you want to focus on collaborative projects. Describe them in one or two sentences, making sure to name the teachers. If you are fortunate enough to have a staff, spotlight any of their accomplishments, such as an eye-catching bulletin board. For rigid schedules, identify achievements by grade level, pointing to any inquiry-based research students did and what they can *do* with the skills they have learned.

Problems that you want to formally call to your administrator's attention can be included in your monthly report. Keep your statements as objective as possible and avoid blaming any person or department. For example, instead of saying that the technology department has not responded to any of your requests for repairs, note that four computers and one printer have not been available to students for the past month. Always include your preferred solution to whatever problem you raise. In this case, you might say that the issue will be resolved as soon as the technology department can send someone to fix the machines.

Circulation statistics are among the least meaningful numbers in today's LMC, but since your administrator expects them, be sure to include them. In a rigid setting, students may automatically borrow two books per week or however often their class is scheduled. Middle and high school students prefer to photocopy endlessly rather than take a book out, so do a table check. (With an automated system, you can scan the books left out and they will be included in your statistics.) Count the titles you put on reserve carts, since these are also being used by teachers and students.

Look for other data that demonstrate the activity of the SLMP. For example, track reference questions. You can set up a daily sheet with boxes for queries relating to location, Internet use, databases, subject areas, and so on. Do not list the actual request; just make tally marks next to the appropriate category as they occur. Enter the totals onto a spreadsheet at the end of the day.

If you are flexibly scheduled, record the grades or the subject area teachers who bring classes to the LMC. Listing each of the sections day by day for the month will result in an extensive report. Although your principal is not likely to read through all of it, the several pages are a visual message of how busy you are and the importance of the SLMP in the school community.

Count students sent to the LMC with passes during the day, as well as those who come before and after school. It is important to call this part of your job to your administrator's attention, since you may be doing far more individualized teaching than she realizes.

In putting your report together, either place the statistical information first or put it on a cover sheet. Administrators love numbers. They put them in their reports and give them to the superintendent and the board of education. Having meaningful ones means that yours will be used and your program will be given broader recognition. After the first year, you can begin including longitudinal data comparing the same month over time. If there is a drop, find a positive way to explain it.

An annual report obviously summarizes what has transpired during the year. Use your monthly reports to compile it. Combine all the statistical data and point out the highlights. For the narrative section, identify the achievements of the SLMP. Include a bulleted list of projections for the following year which may highlight changes you wish to make to the program. You can meet with your principal right after school lets out for vacation to discuss any of these.

Memos

For the most part, e-mail has replaced printed memos. When you do send any printed memos, recognize that their hard-copy format makes them more formal, so whatever you are discussing will have more weight. As with all other forms of communication, be sure to keep them brief and focused.

A good use of the memo format is to call your principal's attention to an item of interest. For example, you might want to inform her of the results of a research project such as those conducted by Keith Curry Lance or the Center for International Studies in School Librarianship that demonstrated the value of an active SLMP, particularly if the study was conducted in your state.[3]

Another example would be if you had a task to complete as the result of a meeting. You would send a memo to update your principal on what you had done and what the results were. As with e-mail, be sure to copy those who were aware of your assignment.

Meetings

Consider all scheduled meetings—other than the brief chats described earlier—to be formal encounters. Bring a pad and pen for notes and any documents that are relevant to the topic under discussion. There may or may not be an official agenda, depending on the level of formality.

Be prompt. Try to avoid being detained, but if you are, be sure to call the secretary with an explanation and the time you think you can arrive. You should not be more than ten minutes late unless there was a dire emergency. Strike a balance between talking too much and not speaking up at all. When you are unsure, restate what you think you heard so that any misconception can be corrected. While you do not want to sound rigid, keep all your remarks focused on the topic under discussion.

On occasion, you may be the one to request a meeting. Do not get annoyed if it is canceled; be prepared to reschedule. Make sure you know the amount of time allotted and keep within it. Follow up within a day or two by sending "minutes" to all who attended. This will serve to fix in everyone's mind what was discussed and decided.

A Matter of Record

What are the best and worst components of your predecessor's reports?

_____

For what aspects of your program will you develop statistics?

_____

What might be the topic of a memo you would send?

_____

What are three important things to remember when attending a meeting?

_____

DOS AND DON'TS

You know that it is highly important to build a strong relationship with your principal—and supervisor if you have one—since obtaining their support is a major contributor to your success. We have reviewed how to manage informal and formal communications, but some points still need to be emphasized. You will be faced with deciding whether to put something in writing or to make a more casual contact. Which format do you use to handle mistakes?

Choosing Your Format

As a general guide, put positive information in writing and use chats as much as possible for problems. You can raise an issue in a monthly report, giving your suggested solution, and then try for a follow-up discussion. If you keep repeating references to the same situation in writing, it will appear that you are creating a paper trail. While there are times when that is the last recourse, you should never undertake it during your first year. You are still establishing your reputation and do not want to seem determined to blame others or be someone who rocks the boat.

Use a few casual chats to keep your principal aware of how well or poorly a problem is being resolved, but be sure to intersperse them with mentions of good things that are happening. You do not want her to see you coming and assume that she is about to be hit with a complaint. That will completely destroy the possibility of getting her support. You should be demonstrating how often you are part of the solution.

As issues begin to work out, send an e-mail to acknowledge the improvement. Thank your principal for her support or advice. Add a comment on occasion as to how much you value her help.

Bringing Bad News

You will make mistakes—everyone does. The temptation is to pretend it never happened and hope it will go away. Depending on what you did, sometimes the best course of action is to face up to it.

Some blunders are library-related and no one, other than you, will pay them much mind. For example, you might have inadvertently ordered two copies of the same book. With a tight budget this is very annoying, but you can chalk it up to the cost of doing business. If it was an expensive reference volume, you will be more upset, but you need not bring it to the attention of your supervisor.

Other gaffes have larger implications. Suppose you said something you should not have to a parent. While there is a chance that she will not take it further, you cannot be sure. First, call her and apologize. Then let your principal know what occurred. Accept responsibility and ask what you should do next. It is far better that you be the one to bring the tale than to discover that the parent went to the superintendent or a board member, who then called your principal.

The key to all this is the recognition that you never want to have something you did catch administrators by surprise. They can deal with problems much better if they know what to expect. You also have the chance to present it in a neutral manner before it is colored with someone else's emotional response.

Watch Your Language

How would you inform your principal that you are feeling ignored by the technology department?

_____

What would you do if you responded sharply to a teacher's complaint about a library practice?

_____

OBSERVATIONS AND EVALUATIONS

Throughout the course of the year your principal or supervisor will observe you both informally and formally. In the latter case, a written report will be made and you will discuss it before it becomes part of your personnel file. If you have a rigid schedule, it is a simple matter for your administrator to choose one of your teaching periods in which to observe you. Those of you who do not see classes at a fixed time will be asked to inform her of when you will be teaching.

In either case, you are bound to be nervous. You can minimize the anxiety by being proactive. Instead of waiting, invite your supervisor to see a class. That way you choose the presentation you want her to see. If you have developed a collaborative lesson, you have a chance to show it off. The teacher will be present and will probably add some positive comments about you.

While you will not be working with a teacher in a rigidly scheduled setting, pick a class that will best show your teaching abilities. In addition to the lesson plan, give your principal a brief handout describing the background for the instruction. Supervisors do not always realize that you are building the current unit on students' past experiences. If you are connecting to a part of the classroom curriculum, say so.

The written report usually contains suggestions for improvement. Do not overreact. In some districts or schools at least one negative comment is standard practice. Supervisors also like to be able to help you do better. During your follow-up conference, accept the comment and be sure you incorporate the recommendation into your teaching and inform your principal of how well it worked. If the comment reflected something that was misconstrued, say that you agree with the idea and then go on to clarify what actually happened.

Since it is your responsibility to help the administrator become familiar with the scope of what you do, suggest some observations that go beyond your teaching. Remind her that your job description includes numerous requirements other than instruction. You can have a conversation about how you want to develop the SLMP, which can be the basis for an observation. Your reports are another possibility. By exploring different means of observing your work, you will be subtly building your principal's understanding of what your job entails.

Near the end of the year, you will be evaluated on your overall performance. Usually this also includes a recommendation for or against rehiring. You can influence the evaluation's content by asking your supervisor if she would like a summary of what you have done. Many supervisors are relieved to have this additional assistance because completing evaluations is a time-consuming task for them.

Create a bulleted list divided into categories to display your accomplishments. Put student learning first. Follow with areas in which you built relationships with staff, parents, and any other members of the educational community. Next focus on what you have done in the LMC to make it a welcoming environment. Complete your account with any professional development you have had, such as attending conferences or serving on committees in school or for state and national associations. As a final item, include the mission of the SLMP.

Being Accountable

Which of your classes would you like your supervisor to observe?

_____

Review your job description. What areas would you like to have included in an observation?

_____

What positive accomplishments are you developing for your end-of-year evaluation?

_____

BUILDING SUPPORT

All of these various forms of communication are paths to encouraging your principal to support the SLMP, but you can go even further in creating that climate. Switch your focus for a moment. Instead of concentrating on getting the administrative cooperation you need, consider why your supervisor should help you. The answers to that question suggest where you should put extra effort.

Being Supportive

As Mahatma Gandhi reportedly said, "You must be the change you want to see in the world." If you want to get support, show that you can give it. Although new ideas take hold slowly in education, the administration usually introduces something each year. It may be as simple as a different way to do lesson plans or a more challenging task such as using a new piece of software in tracking student progress. Whatever it is, be among those who embrace the change.

As previously noted, even small schools have factions that are for or against the administration. The latter are automatically opposed to anything the principal suggests. You can be a big help by being quietly supportive. A comment as to the minimal change required by the new lesson plan, for example, or doing a one-on-one demonstration of the software to ease a teacher's anxiety can smooth the adoption of the innovation. Not only will the principal be appreciative of your assistance, but you will also be furthering your relationship with the faculty.

Although "being a team player" is an overused phrase, the concept is important. If you are seen as being part of the solution rather than another problem, it is in the interest of your principal to help build your program. You want to be someone she can trust. Eventually this will lead to more frequent chats that allow you to share your vision for where you want to take the SLMP with a receptive audience.

Sharing Common Perspectives

Before you bring your vision to your principal, figure out what hers is. What is she trying to achieve? Whether it is improving test scores or involving parents, you can adapt your aims to align with hers without minimizing or losing sight of your own. When you can show your administrator how the SLMP can advance her goals, you will get support for your program.

As your chats with the principal become more frequent, build on the unique perspective you share. Neither of you is tied to a subject or grade level. You both interact with students over the years and enjoy watching them grow. Unless you have a co-librarian, each of you is the sole representative of your profession in the building. People rarely see the full scope of your responsibilities but have lots of expectations for what you can and should do. With so much in common, you have the basis for building a relationship that will be helpful to you both.

Although it is normal to be somewhat apprehensive about dealing with your administrator (she is the one to determine whether or not you will be rehired), you will be more successful if you approach her as a potential ally. Just as you became acquainted with your teachers, get to know your principal. Without imposing on her own heavy responsibilities, gradually educate her as to the scope of your job and the correlation of an active SLMP with student achievement. When supervisors see how you benefit them and the school program, you get the support you need.

Giving a Hand, Getting a Hand

What is the school goal for the year? What can you do to support it?

_____

What interests does your principal have? Do you share any of them?

_____

What do you think is your administrator's vision?

_____

Key Ideas

- Support from your principal or supervisor is a critical factor in the success of the SLMP.
- Speak as the expert you are.
- Do not bring up important issues when your administrator drops by unannounced in your LMC.
- Chats you initiate with your principal should be about relatively simple matters.
- Limit your conversation to the agreed-upon time and be concise and informative.
- If you are criticized, show that you are eager to learn and improve.
- Reports should contain significant statistics that can be compared from one year to the next.
- Narrative sections of reports should focus on student achievement.
- Keep memos as short as possible.
- Talk about problems with your principal rather than putting them in writing.
- Own up to mistakes that might land on an administrator's desk.
- Invite your supervisor to observe one of your lessons.
- Suggest areas other than teaching for future observations.
- Offer to make a list of what you did during the year to help your supervisor prepare your final evaluation.
- Show support in order to get it.
- Align your vision with the principal's.

NOTES

1. Anthony F. Gregorc, *Gregorc Style Delineator: Development, Technical, and Administration Manual* (New York: Gabriel Systems, 1984). See also "Gregorc Associates Inc.," http://www.gregorc.com.
2. American Association of School Librarians, Association for Educational Communications and Technology, *Information Power: Building Partnerships for Learning* (Chicago: American Library Association, 1998), 4–5.
3. Information on studies done by Keith Curry Lance can be found at http://www.lrs.org/impact.asp, and those conducted by the Center for International Studies in School Librarianship are at http://www.cissl.scils.rutgers.edu.

CHAPTER 8

Advocacy and You

It's wise to flock together.

*S*everal years ago, advocacy moved from the concept of promoting an issue—such as "advocating for school reform"—to being an initiative many organizations have embraced. A number of people regarded it as just another buzzword for doing the same old thing, but those who were open to learning more soon realized it was quite different and very powerful. In today's world where jobs are based on increased accountability, knowing how to incorporate advocacy into what you do has become necessary to your survival.

WHAT ADVOCACY IS

Before you can use it, you need to understand what advocacy is and is not. There is a tendency to confuse it with public relations and marketing. In practice, those two activities join advocacy to form a tripod on which to showcase your program.

Becoming clear about the differences and functions of these three practices is important since you will be using each of them. In general, think of public relations as short-term, marketing as a fixed-period campaign, and advocacy as an ongoing way of being. Sometimes you will have all three going at once. But no matter what else you are or are not doing, you will always be advocating at some level.

Public Relations

This can be the easiest of the three activities to use. Simply put, public relations tells people what you are doing well. You let them know of your existence and show that you provide an important service.

Some examples of good public relations are to invite people to an event you are holding in the library media center, or announce a new database that you will demonstrate. It can even be as simple as making sure the hours the LMC is open are posted in a visible location. If you are so inclined (and can manage to fit it into your very crowded schedule), try to do something every month to keep people aware of the school library media program.

Once you understand what public relations is, you realize how much of it you already do. You distribute bookmarks or create a brochure about the LMC. Perhaps you hand out pencils with the library's name on them. Now that you are conscious of it, keep track of all these mini-campaigns and inform your principal about them.

If you would like to get some possible ideas for a public relations program, check out the winners of the John Cotton Dana Award by going to http://www.ala.org, clicking on "Awards and Scholarships," and scrolling down until you reach this link. Sponsored by the H. W. Wilson Company, the award honors an outstanding library public relations program. While public libraries are the most frequent recipients of the award, finding out what they did may suggest possibilities for something you might want to try in the future.

Marketing

Marketing is about selling your program and is an area that the ALA is newly stressing. As with public relations, your campaign can be small or large—and for your first attempt you want to take a baby step. Once you get positive results, you will be eager to try another. Just remember, do not offer more than you can deliver.

To have a successful marketing campaign, you need to determine just what you want to sell and what message to use. The easiest approach is to latch on to what the ALA has already developed and use the "@ your library" brand with your own slogan. You can even find clever slogans readymade on the website.

Go to http://www.ala.org/ala/pio/campaign/campaignamericas.htm and click on "School Library Campaign." The first available document is a 53-page toolkit loaded with ideas. Look for slogans appropriate by grade level and examples of how the brand has been used in different places. Print out the document in PDF and keep it handy in a three-ring binder.

Decide whether you want to use one slogan throughout your campaign (as in "Got Milk?") or vary them to keep up interest. Think of your slogans as highlighting a four-step process. Initially you want to raise *awareness*. What is happening in the LMC that key stakeholders should know about? (A bit of public relations is important here.)

Next you want your target audience to develop *interest*. Tease them into taking a closer look. Once they are hooked, raise their *desire* for the service. Show why it is something they cannot live without. Finally, present them with an opportunity to take *action*. In the business world, this is where you make the sale. What do you want them to do?

While selling your program is essential, don't think you must create a grand campaign. Principals and teachers have to be aware of what you do and why it is important to them. On the other hand, developing a marketing campaign requires time to think through the steps and develop all the parts and a timeline to execute it.

Eventually you may want to work with the other SLMSs in your district on a campaign. Your state affiliate may put on training sessions using ALA materials to teach you how to construct a detailed campaign. Until then, just let everyone know that "Every Student Succeeds @ your library."

Advocacy

As noted earlier, advocacy is a continuing process. Look for partners and recognize that aspects of your success are intertwined with theirs. If you are in an elementary school with a rigid schedule, you have something in common with the art, music, and physical education teachers. They would also like to connect to the curriculum.

Instead of each of you working in your separate areas, find ways to work together for a greater impact. For your initial effort, tie your collaboration to the school calendar. You might prepare a schoolwide Thanksgiving celebration. Students can learn art forms as they decorate the building depicting the theme, study songs related to the holiday, and play old-fashioned games in gym. For *your* contribution, help students research the history of the feast and find and make colonial recipes. Read stories to them about the day and about gratitude. A showcase from all four areas just before vacation will do much to focus attention on the contribution you all make to increase student learning.

The AASL provides a PowerPoint training that will help you tailor an advocacy campaign for your school. Go to http://www.ala.org/aasl/, click on "Issues and Advocacy," and scroll down for the presentation. Notice that the terms *public relations, marketing,* and *advocacy* are used almost interchangeably here. As long as you are aware of what you are doing and what you are trying to achieve, the term itself does not matter.

You need not spend time each day or even once a week on advocacy. What you must do is make it part of your way of doing business. While it is important to let others know what you do that is unique, keep promoting *their* work *which you support through the SLMP.* As they come to rely on your assistance, they have a stake in your survival. And you must have a stake in theirs. That is advocacy.

Promoting Your Program

What small public relations idea can bring your program to teachers' attention?

_____

What part of your program do you want to sell? Who is the prime audience?

_____

How can you connect with the school nurse? The computer teacher?

_____

What other partnerships can you create in your building?

_____

WHY YOU NEED IT

Teaching students and managing the administrative aspects of the LMC is a huge job. Added to that is your responsibility for developing collaborative relationships with teachers and making your principal aware of the scope of what you do. With all that on your plate, when are you going to find time for public relations, marketing, and advocacy? Is it really that important?

Yes, it is that important, but as was stated earlier, you are already doing a lot of it. In encouraging collaboration with teachers, you are constantly engaged in marketing. As noted in chapter 6, they feel they are very successful without the SLMP. You are the one who shows them how their students can learn more when you work together. You offer them support at whatever level they will accept, hoping they will come to realize how much they need you. That is marketing.

Your reports to your principal, whether required or not, are public relations. You are letting her know what is happening in the LMC. Posters announcing special services or new databases are also public relations.

What you are probably not doing much of is advocacy. In your first months on the job, you have a great deal to assimilate and little time to focus on creating partnerships. But on your calendar or wherever you will notice it, make a note that somewhere in the third marking period you should begin to think about advocacy.

We live in a world of tight budgets and accountability. No matter what the economy does, this will not change. Every department in the district is fighting for money and staff. To maintain and build a strong program, you need a lot of support. If your focus is on *defending* your needs, you will find each year the administration chips a little bit away. It is a losing battle.

Stop worrying about guarding your territory, put your energy into creating alliances, and your program will thrive. In his bestseller, *The World Is Flat,* Thomas L. Friedman discusses a fundamental change in how economies work. Although he is describing the business world, the message applies equally well in the education setting. He observes that we are moving from a vertical, command and control model to a horizontal, connect and collaborate model.[1] Connecting and collaborating are the hallmarks of advocacy.

Focus on your goals and outcomes. Who else shares them? What can you do together that would be more successful than if you worked separately? It is natural for an SLMS to think, "How can I help you?" Use this mind-set when speaking with everyone in the educational community. The more people who know who you are and what the SLMP can do for them, the more likely you are to find supporters when you need them.

By continually reaching out to others, you also get a reputation for being a team player. As noted earlier, the term is overused, but it is not bad when the administration perceives you that way. Give a lot before asking for support in return, but be prepared to ask for help when you need it. When you do, make your request specific and key it to your common goals.

Creating an Advocacy Program

What public relations are you already doing?

_____

What marketing are you doing?

_____

List your goals and outcomes. Who shares them in whole or in part?

_____

AVOIDING PITFALLS

While advocacy and its "handmaidens"—public relations and marketing—are important to keep in mind, we cannot state too often that you should move slowly when in a new job situation. Cliques, rivalries, and friendships are already in place, and you will have little knowledge for some time about where these lines are drawn. If you are fortunate enough to have a clerk or active volunteers, they may start filling you in as you build a relationship with them. Until then, steer clear of major projects in this area.

One of the most common missteps is to speak at a faculty meeting about a problem you are experiencing or an action step you want to take. It seems like such a logical idea. Everyone is together; you can prepare your thoughts. What could be simpler?

Before you open your mouth, reflect on what is happening at this time. It is after school. People are tired. Some are griping about the length of the agenda. Others use this as an opportunity to make negative comments about the administration to a friend sitting next to them. Then you step up with your great plan. What reception are you going to get?

Although a few might ask questions, most teachers do not want to drag this out. The sooner you are finished, the earlier the meeting will end. What is worse, the naysayers are dissecting your idea, pointing out what is wrong with it (or you for suggesting it) to those alongside them. *And you will not hear any of this.* All you will discover is that you have a low level of cooperation, and you will start getting frustrated.

Instead of launching your campaign at a faculty meeting, test it out with those teachers you trust. Listen to what they have to say. Tinker with it. Try it with a few others. If you must present it to the whole group, have your support already built up. Let everyone know that you have spoken with a number of people and you want to thank them for their input. Do not mention names, since that can cause another set of problems.

If any of your projects involve money, be sure you know if and where it is available. Do not assume that having money in your budget means you can spend it on what you like. Accounts are reserved for special purposes (see chapter 9), and not all expenditures are permitted.

Speak with your principal to ensure you proceed according to district policies. Focus on what you hope to achieve, why it is important, and how you plan to accomplish it. Discuss your anticipated budget and have a smaller, cheaper version to fall back on if your first suggestion is not accepted. By demonstrating that you plan for contingencies, you are more likely to get approval.

Usually, you also need permission for fund-raising activities. Find out who oversees this area and learn what steps are required. Because you are accustomed to working alone, making choices about book orders and other aspects of managing the LMC, you can easily act as though you are an independent operator. However, projects that occur frequently during the year under the auspices of teachers (or parents), such as bake sales, are normally more closely regulated. Always check to be sure you are not violating school or district procedures.

Treading with Caution

What patterns and behaviors have you observed during faculty meetings?

_____

Which teachers would you speak to before addressing the faculty?

_____

How would you request a meeting with your principal to discuss an advocacy, public relations, or marketing project?

_____

TALKING WITH PARENTS AND SCHOOL BOARD MEMBERS

One of the best and worst aspects of your job is that—within the limits of school security—there is open access to you and the LMC. Although you customarily think of open access in terms of students and teachers being able to come to the LMC as needed, the phrase frequently embraces other members of the educational community. Chapter 7 discussed how to manage when the principal (or even the superintendent of schools) drops by unannounced, but you should also anticipate school board members and parents (sometimes wearing both hats) visiting your facility.

Volunteers

If you are at the elementary school level, volunteers may be your only support staff. You will need to recruit, train, and hold on to them. Most often these are parents of your students, although senior citizens and grandparents may be among your helpers.

Since they are not being paid, volunteers need other motivators to bring them in and keep them coming back. On the most positive side, their motive is to help make their children's school a better place. A degree of curiosity is normally present as well. In some cases, there is a desire to ensure that their child is getting the best teachers, preferential treatment, and that educational practices conform to their viewpoint. Managing all these can be a challenge but is well worth your time and effort.

Whether the volunteers sought you out, worked in the LMC previously, or responded to an invitation from you to come to a tea in the media center, once you have them you need to get the most from them. You do this by making them feel valued. Greet them when they arrive and thank them when they leave. Give your regulars ongoing jobs for which they can be solely responsible. These can be as simple as weeding and shelf reading a section that connects to their special area of knowledge, or more specialized tasks such as entering students into the database, doing simple cataloging, and so on.

While you do want volunteers to handle clerical and even para-professional tasks, you should not have them take on professional ones unless you are fortunate enough to have someone with a library background. For example, one new SLMS allowed parents to do story time with classes while she checked in books. The balance of responsibilities was completely skewed, and it resulted in a major mess. The SLMS divided her time between buildings. One day when she was at another school, her volunteers—who felt they could handle anything—decided to reclassify books. They put a significant number of beginning reader nonfiction in with the picture books. As they only changed spine labels, locating the titles was a time-consuming task. In addition, she had to ease hurt feelings, while establishing procedures to reign in overly exuberant helpers.

You need to have ground rules for acceptable practices. Go over them during the tea and on their first visit when you are training new volunteers. As much as possible, do not change what was previously allowed. Is it acceptable for young children to come with their mothers? (If you do not permit this, you may lose many potential helpers.) Are there a minimum number of hours per week required? Can they schedule themselves to be there when their child has library? (This is a big draw.)

How much authority are you going to give volunteers to discipline students? If you are not in the school full-time, you will need to give them some responsibility in this area. Speak about your philosophy and offer some scenarios as to how you would want them handled. Listen to the volunteers' opinions and work with them.

Volunteers tend to chatter among themselves. If they get too loud—and they sometimes do—have a discussion that alerts them to what is happening without making them feel "wrong." Let them know that teachers sometimes do this as well. When people get to talking, it is easy to forget voice levels.

Since some of your helpers are there for the social aspects, you want to be sure you are still getting work from them. Make a list of tasks that you want done for the day and have them initial what they accomplished. If you compliment the hard workers publicly, the others will get the idea.

In addition to being extra pairs of hands, your volunteers are your eyes, ears—and mouths—in the community. If you do not live locally, they are the ones who will keep you posted on what is happening and give you some inside information. They can also be your best supporters as they report to friends and neighbors about the learning that occurs in the LMC. Be sure to take time to explain to them about information literacy, current research on the connection between active SLMPs and student achievement, and the varied roles you play.

At the same time, be cautious when speaking with your volunteers. Never criticize the administration or any teachers. Your comments will be repeated and will come back to haunt you. Whenever possible, put a positive spin on any negatives they observe. In one elementary school, a volunteer observed how often the students in one class needed to be reminded to behave. She commented, "Mrs. Z. is not a very good teacher." The SLMS, who was familiar with the situation, responded, "Mrs. Z. is really an excellent teacher with a number of challenging special needs students in her class."

If you find yourself in a difficult situation, such as a budget cut, there is a temptation to marshal your volunteers to wield their influence. Even if you are apparently successful, your reputation with the administration will be harmed. You can let your supporters know what is happening, but do not suggest a course of action to them. Anything they choose to do must be their own decision. You may have to curtail some of their more extreme plans, but make sure that you cannot be seen as encouraging them. (For more information about working with volunteers and planning for their successful participation, see chapter 9.)

Parents

Even if they are not volunteers, parents will occasionally come to the LMC. Sometimes they want to complain about how you treated their child or discuss a problem with a lost or overdue book. They may want suggestions for reading material, or occasionally they wish to register a complaint about a book. You will want to handle each of these situations with care.

Two guidelines should help you get through the first examples. First, listen actively to what is being said. Do not interrupt or work on what your response will be while the parent is talking. Restate what you believe you heard to be sure that you both agree with what the situation is. Second, do not be defensive. State your policy and practices as objectively as possible, observing that these are uniformly enforced. Ask what the parents' expectations are. Explain what you plan to do (or not do), including informing the principal who can either overrule or uphold your decision.

If parents wish to have a book removed from the shelves, keep calm as recommended in chapter 4. Compliment them on being caring and conscientious. Although you should have a selection policy in place and be prepared to give them the form you use for challenged material, see if you can keep things from escalating to that point. With today's automated circulation systems, you can usually put a comment in a child's record indicating that he is not permitted certain books. Offer that option, pointing out that parents have full authority to control what their child has access to, but restricting other children is a different matter.

Whatever the situation, how you handle it will be a learning experience for the parents. They will find out more about the SLMP, its place in the school, and what it means for students and teachers. Rather than feeling attacked, focus on any of these occurrences as an opportunity to promote your program.

Board Members

While some districts do not permit school board members free access to the schools, you may find it is acceptable or even encouraged where you are. In some cases, the board members may be your volunteer parents. It is usually a good idea to learn board members' names and know if they have children in your school. Not that you will give them preferential treatment, but you should be aware of who they are in case a circumstance arises that might get reported home.

Treat visiting board members the same way you handle an appearance by your principal. If you are involved with a class or working with a student, do not stop. However, if you are not engaged in teaching, interrupt what you are doing and welcome them. Ask what you can do to help and respond to their questions.

When you become more familiar with some of them, you can speak of accomplishments and plans, focusing on the successes of students and teachers. By now you should know that you do not use their visit to complain. Even if they should bring up an issue, be careful how you respond. For example, in one school a number of computers had "out of order" signs on them. The board had met in the LMC, and this particular member saw the notices and wanted to know what was happening. The answer was, "We are waiting for them to be repaired. The principal is aware of the situation and is dealing with it."

Whether or not the board member focused on a problem area or was just looking around, be sure to notify your administrator of the visit. You cannot predict how this encounter will be relayed, and you want to make sure that your principal is not caught by surprise.

Extending Advocacy

What does this section have to do with advocacy?

_____

What guidelines will you have for volunteers?

_____

What do you want your volunteers to know about the SLMP? How will they learn it?

_____

What is the first thing you will say to a parent who brings a complaint to you?

_____

What are the names of your school board members?

_____

SPEAKING OUTSIDE THE SCHOOL

On occasion, you may speak with those not directly connected to the school. You might visit other local libraries or an organization that works with a segment of your student body. Perhaps you are asked to address a parent-teacher group or the business community. In each case, you need to think about the focus of your message and how to use the meeting to strengthen support for your program.

Other Libraries

Get to know the staff of the local public library. Know the names of the librarians and the rest of the people who work there. Some may have children in your school. Your message, voiced or not, is "We are partners." Exchange e-mail addresses so you can quickly alert them to projects occurring in your school, and they can contact you if they need to know what a particular teacher wants her students to discover. Invite the children's librarian (or the young adult or reference librarian if you are in a middle or high school) to visit you.

Find out what databases you have in common and which are unique. If an interlibrary loan system is not in place, you may be able to set up a personal one, requesting materials for teachers and students—and allowing the public library to borrow books from your collection not connected to a current assignment. By drawing on each other's strengths you will do a better job, and you can show the community that you are making maximum use of its tax dollars.

Secondary school SLMSs should also make the acquaintance of any academic librarians in their area. The push is to look at information literacy at levels K–20, so it helps if you can open a dialogue with them about what abilities their professors find lacking in entering freshmen. You can then design lessons to build those missing skills. Your teachers will be more apt to collaborate with you if they learn that you have opened this channel and are working to ensure their students' college success.

Community Organizations

Whether it is a YMCA or a place where poverty-level children spend a great deal of time, try to learn more about the community resources your students use. With all you have to do, you may not have an opportunity to meet with these organizations until spring or later, but be mindful of their existence and try to schedule a meeting before school resumes the following year.

As with other libraries, invite key people to visit your facility, but in this case expect the cooperation to be mostly one-sided. You want to develop a sense of the places where a number of your students may be after school. If these places have computers available, check with your database providers and see if your license allows them to have the passwords to access these resources off-site. Let the vendors know that this may be the only way some students can use the databases because home connections are not available.

Parent Groups

Whether you are trying to increase the number of regular volunteers, get help for a special event such as a book fair, or just want to show parents what they need to know about Internet use, speak to the parent organization in your school. Be warmly professional in your demeanor and open to requests and inquiries no matter what the purpose of your talk.

Always have a handout to distribute. Cull your latest statistics to illustrate the vitality of the SLMP; include "fast facts" about libraries which you can get from the various toolkits available at the AASL website; list recommended alternate search engines; and inform parents of the electronic databases which they can also access. Use your best design skills in preparing the handout, and list your e-mail and phone number so that you can be reached with questions afterward.

Everyone loves freebies, so in addition to the handout you might consider distributing one of your public relations items. Pencils are great, but if your budget does not stretch that far, offer informative bookmarks that you either purchased or made. Although preparing these items as well as your talk will add to your already overburdened schedule, you will not be doing it that often, and you need to make the most of your opportunity. The handout can become a boilerplate for others that you make, so the investment will pay off over time.

Business Organizations

In addition to the parent groups, there are times when you want to approach local businesses. You might be asking them to give you computers when they upgrade their machines or to volunteer for a read-in. You will most likely be speaking at a Kiwanis or Rotary meeting. Although you would have discussed the project far in advance with your principal and gotten permission for your plans, you will also need to get release time, since these meetings are invariably held at midday and their lunches last much longer than the ones that schools schedule.

Again, you want to have a handout to give them. In addition to the items suggested for parents, you will want to stress that information literacy skills prepare students to think through problems and be ready to learn new things. The business world is not looking for graduates who can do the current job but ones who are able to quickly adjust to a fast-changing environment. You want to show them—succinctly—that the SLMP provides this "value-added" commodity in the educational setting.

Even if you are not asking them to come to the school for a specific event, extend an invitation to them to visit the LMC. A few might take you up on your offer, and you can show them how much today's LMC differs from the school libraries they knew when they were young. Always remember that they are taxpayers who, in many states, vote on the school budget.

Reaching Out to the Community

What colleges are in your area?

_____

What organizations serve the disenfranchised in the community?

_____

What are some possible topics for a talk you might give to the parent association?

_____

What would you like from local businesses? What can you offer them in return?

_____

MANAGING THE MEDIA

SLMSs look for opportunities to get local newspapers or television outlets to cover a library event, but most of the time they are unsuccessful. Here as in other areas, you need to build a relationship in order to get results. Find out which person is in charge of education news at the local paper or television station. Send e-mails to these people commenting on columns or programs that you admired.

Well before you ask reporters to come to the LMC to cover a story, find out how far in advance you need to inform the newspaper or station about the event. (You can make reminder calls as necessary.) Also, discuss what types of situations will bring them to the school. Invariably, journalists want to have pictures of students (and you will need to know what release forms are required). With contacts already in place, when you do invite them to attend some LMC happening, you will be able to present it in a way that is most likely to get you the desired coverage.

The flip side of successfully bringing the media into the LMC is that you will be interviewed. Although you will be asked many questions, only a small part of your answers will be used, and you want to be sure that you cannot be quoted as saying anything negative that reflects on the school or the staff. You can promote the goals of the SLMP, but show how these are achieved as a result of administrative support and teacher collaboration. Highlight student successes. In other words, have only positive things to say.

Media Manners

What are the local newspapers and who has the education beat on them?

_____

How often do school events make news? Do you see any patterns?

_____

What local television stations cover schools? Is there one person who does most of the reporting?

_____

VENDOR RELATIONS

It may seem odd to discuss vendors in a chapter on advocacy, but they can be an overlooked source of support. You deal with two types, and they can each benefit you in different ways. The ones that visit on-site know what is happening in your area and can provide news as well as alert you to new resources. Large companies from whom you purchase supplies and services often have free materials that can improve the look of your facility or help you advertise the latest acquisitions.

Periodically, a sales representative may call on you. (In some districts this is prohibited, but see what can be done because they provide a valuable service.) Rigidly scheduled SLMSs have to meet with them at the end of the school day, but those of you who have the flexibility can see them whenever you are not teaching a class.

Some SLMSs refuse to speak with vendors, claiming they only want to sell their products. Of course they do! And you want to buy them—not everything, but the ones that meet the needs of your students and teachers. When they show up, they bring you copies of books to look over. This is a better way of making a purchasing decision than reading reviews by other people. In addition, you can show the titles to any teachers who are present and get their opinion—and engage their interest.

Good sales representatives come to know your collection and your curriculum and focus on titles they think will work for you. They need to do this if they are going to make a sale, but at the same time it helps you. Most keep track of your past purchases to prevent you from duplicate ordering. However, you will need to be careful not to buy books from your jobber (see chapter 9) that you have already ordered from the representative. Since sales representatives limit themselves to particular publishers, when reading reviews mark the ones you will want to purchase from your rep.

As you examine the items, you can chat about what is going on in the region. You might hear that someone is changing their library automation system or that a nearby SLMS is leaving at the end of the year. (You may or may not be interested in possible job openings elsewhere.) Once you have completed your selection, many sales representatives will prepare the order list for you so that you need only attach it to your purchase order. You can delete any items that on reconsideration you decide not to buy.

Large companies, particularly database vendors, often have posters and other items that promote their products and will send you these to alert students and teachers to what is available. Some have teacher and student guides which include lesson plans that can be used directly or be adapted.

Their websites also have numerous free resources. Since these frequently change, check in whenever you have a few spare moments. You can often get good ideas or ask for a demo of a product that you think will fill a need. Speak with someone in their sales and marketing departments and find out if they will send a representative to do an in-person demonstration. They will often provide a trainer for a staff development day at no charge.

In Favor of Vendors

Do your LMC's past purchase orders indicate any acquisitions from publisher representatives?

_____

What resources, if any, are available on the websites of your database vendors?

_____

Which databases would you like to have demonstrated?

_____

Key Ideas

- Public relations is putting a spotlight on what you do.
- Marketing is creating a need for your program.
- Advocacy is a continuous process of giving and getting support from a broad range of people.
- Be conscious of your public relations and marketing strategies.
- Look for partners.
- Do not address the faculty unless you have done the groundwork first.
- Verify that you can use money in your budget for advocacy projects.
- Learn the procedures for fund-raising activities.
- Volunteers are your connection to the community.
- Respond positively when challenged by parents.
- Treat school board members the same way you treat your principal.
- Identify various groups outside the school with whom you can make connections.
- With administrative approval, create an open door policy and invite members of these groups to visit the LMC.
- Always have a handout to distribute when speaking to community groups.
- Become acquainted with newspaper and television reporters who cover local school events.
- Be careful what you say to reporters.

NOTE

1. Thomas L. Friedman, *The World Is Flat: A Brief History of the Twenty-First Century* (New York: Farrar, Straus and Giroux, 2005), 201.

CHAPTER 9

Planning

This would be much simpler if I could get everything I want.

*N*o matter what task you undertake in the library media center, you need to operate from a plan. You might be doing something as basic as shifting shelves to eliminate tightly packed books or as complex as considering a renovation of the LMC. In the first example you see where there are relatively open spaces and calculate at which point to begin moving books. (You will get better at estimating as you become more experienced.) The second instance is rarer and not likely to occur when you are fairly new, but the situation may arise and you must be ready.

Sometimes you take over an LMC and know there are urgent needs which must be tackled, but in most places things are working well enough. The thought of taking precious and rare moments to plan does not seem to be the best use of your time, but you should be prepared.

On occasion, money just materializes and you are expected to spend it quickly and wisely. Grants obtained by another department might require media center resources. School boards that had been foot-dragging may have recently elected members who decide that the long-delayed library automation project must begin now or that collections need updating. Perhaps a new technology plan is implemented which includes additional equipment for the LMC. What do you want to purchase? Do you know where to get it? Are supporting items required? In other words, what is your plan?

CREATING A PLAN

All planning should stem from your vision for the school library media program. Way back in chapter 1, we noted that vision is about how you wish the LMC to be perceived, and we briefly discussed the sometimes-blurred distinctions between your vision, your philosophy, and your mission. At that time we quoted from the vision in *Information Power* which has the SLMP playing a "unique and pivotal role in the learning community" and is "based on three central ideas: collaboration, leadership, and technology."[1]

If there is no existing vision or you are not comfortable with the one you inherited, start by jotting down terms that express what you want your SLMP to be. Once you have these key words, turn them into two or three sentences. Keep it brief enough to fit on a small sign where it will be visible to you and others. Although you can create the first draft on your own, share it with any of your support staff, including volunteers as well as teachers with whom you are building a relationship. Ask for their input.

Setting Goals

Once your vision is relatively polished, begin to set goals. Mentally scan all aspects of the SLMP and the LMC, making a list of areas that you want to improve to realize that vision. Does the book collection need attention? Are you still using a print catalog? Do you want to develop a better relationship with teachers in a department or grade level?

You will not complete formulating your goals in one sitting. The best time for writing them is probably at the end of the school day. When things have quieted down, relax, reflect, and begin your notes. After you have identified several areas needing improvement, craft them into goal statements such as: "To weed outdated material from the collection." In the back of your mind, add "so that" and complete the sentence by tying it to your vision. For example, this goal statement might continue with: "it is consistent with the curriculum, to bring about collaboration."

Assign priorities to your goals so you see where to concentrate your efforts. Determine this by balancing critical needs with what is most achievable in your first year. Also think about the extent to which achieving this goal would further your vision.

Share these plans with your administrator, along with the action steps (see below) that you create. In sharing your goals and the strategies for achieving them, you have an opening for explaining your roles and the benefits of the SLMP. The discussion will give the administrator a better understanding of how you manage your job and may be the basis for a non-teaching observation by her.

Developing Action Steps

Once you have established your goals, list what you need to do to accomplish them. For example, if you are going to weed the collection, do not start with the 000s and work forward. Choose the section that is in greatest need of weeding. You might even break it down into the next level of subdivisions, such as the 910s.

Make a table (or a spreadsheet) with the goal on top and your action steps below. Next to each step, have a column for assigning the date when you expect to complete the task. Be as realistic as possible. Accept that some of your goals will take more than one year to finish. Put the "due date" in pencil on a large monthly calendar so that you remind yourself often of what you are planning to accomplish. The penciling is to give you some wiggle room when you discover how difficult it is to fit in these jobs.

If you have *any* support staff, paid or volunteer, use a third column to indicate who will be doing the job. Even professional tasks may have clerical or paraprofessional aspects which can be assigned to others. Establish guidelines for the project so that one or more persons can work on it. For example, let volunteers begin the weeding process by pulling books from shelves. You might tell them to remove anything over fifteen years old or whatever looks dated. Have them place these on a cart or on top of a display-height bookcase for you to review. If you need to return some of their choices, take a few minutes to explain to your helpers why you are doing so.

Although weeding is a common goal and there are many good reasons why you might want to have your staff assist on the project, you should also get directly involved. You need opportunities to become familiar with the collection in order to help students and collaborate with teachers. You almost never have time to read shelves to be sure the books are in order, but you will get to know what you have if you begin weeding.

Managing Large Plans

You may find yourself faced with a huge—possibly even a multiyear—project. It may be a renovation of the LMC, the construction of a new facility, or a library automation project. If you are not the person who initiated the project, be sure to get copies of all the paperwork on it, including memos and e-mail (if available) from the time the concept was begun to its present state. Make time to speak with everyone who has any knowledge of the undertaking. Find out their understanding of its purpose, anticipated results, and individual responsibilities. Your object is to learn the project's current status and what you are expected to do. Put everything in a file (preferably digital) with subsets for major sections.

Large plans are considered capital expenditures. The rules concerning these are somewhat different from other purchases. Be sure you know the procedures. For example, if you are doing a renovation project, you will need furniture and shelving. Can you stipulate that everything must be supplied by one vendor, or does the district accept partial bids? You will probably prefer the former situation so as to avoid getting items that do not look good together. If you are doing a library automation project, can you state that you are dealing with proprietary software, so you will not have to select the low bidder but instead base your choice on the results of a request for proposal (RFP), similar to the way textbooks are chosen?

Set up a rough timeline of when components need to be completed. Identify your contacts for these steps. If furniture needs to be ordered, are you making the choice or are you selecting from an approved list of suppliers? Is there an architect with whom you can speak, and are you permitted to suggest changes? Are vendors allowed to provide assistance even though most of the items will have to go out to bid?

If you are involved with a library automation project, most likely all the schools are doing it, or you are following a preset sequence to get buildings online. See which SLMSs have preceded you in the sequence, or contact the others in the district to be sure you are all following a similar plan.

To keep track of the project without becoming overwhelmed and stressed out, fluctuate between *microscoping, periscoping,* and *telescoping.* Spend most of your time in the *microscope* phase, focusing on the immediate job and its due date. About once a week send up a *periscope* to see what is coming next so that you are ready to go. Depending on the size of the project, at least once a month look through the *telescope* to recall other components with which you will have to deal. The purpose of this is to remind you of what will be occurring in the next months and alert you to glitches. For example, you may realize you should have received a notice about something that will be happening in a few weeks. Discovering this early gives you a chance to check on what is holding things up, find out what needs to be done to clear the path, and perhaps adjust your timeline.

Whether you are creating a plan for a large or small project, always share it with your staff and ask for input. Some of their suggestions will be valuable and others will not work. Thank them for their contribution— even if you cannot use everything. Explain your reasoning to those whose recommendations you are not taking, but let them know that their looking for ways to do things better and more efficiently is a great help to you.

Project Planning

What are some words you want to include in your vision statement?

_____

What are three areas in the SLMP or LMC that you want to improve?

_____

Is there a large project that is being or should be done? When is it scheduled for completion, or when would you like to get it started?

_____

MONEY MATTERS

Budget planning may have been discussed while you were in library school, but that was either a hypothetical construct or one you borrowed. In either case, it was not real. Once you are in your own LMC, the prospect of developing a budget, which you may have to do within weeks of starting the school year, can be an intimidating prospect. Even an experienced SLMS who has changed schools can be concerned when faced with making decisions while having little background on what is needed.

In addition to planning the budget, at some point you may want to find other sources of money. You will need to know and weigh your options as part of your planning process. This will help you determine where to look for funding.

Budget Process

Every school district has a budget cycle, which is generally regulated by the state. Most commonly, fiscal years begin the month after school ends, but find out what the practice is where you are. Inevitably, you are in the middle of a cycle when you arrive, and you will be asked to prepare a budget for the next one. Depending on when it is due, you may have little time to get ready.

To get yourself grounded, review a copy of the current library budget. If it was not in your files, ask the principal's secretary where you can get one. Also request a printout of the status of your budget for this fiscal year. You want to know the amount appropriated, in what accounts, what has been expended, and how much remains.

Look over the documents and make a list of questions. Find out who can help you with them and schedule a meeting. You may notice there are two different totals. One is for the amount encumbered and the other is what has already been spent.

For beginners, the concept of "encumbered" funds can be confusing. When a purchase order is generated and signed off by the appropriate parties, it goes to the accounting department where the total amount is encumbered—deducted from the money you have available to spend, although nothing has been paid out as yet. When you sign the PO, reporting that the items have been received, accounts payable sends a check to the vendor. The exact dollar figure may be higher or lower than the PO, since items may have been canceled or cost slightly more or less than anticipated, and shipping and handling charges might be somewhat different from the original calculation. Once the vendor has been paid, the sum is removed from the encumbered column and deducted from what you have left to spend.

What is most important is that you really do not have as much money as you think. You must deduct the total encumbered funds from what has been expended in order to know what you really have left.

Another common practice in schools is to "sweep accounts" after a certain date. This means the administration will take all funds remaining and put them in a surplus account or use them for other purposes. Ask the school secretary if this is usually done and when you can anticipate it occurring. You will have to spend all your money before that time, not only to purchase everything you want for the LMC but also to ensure that your budget is not reduced next year. Some districts operate on the principle that if the money was not used, you do not need that much, and they deduct the amount not spent from your budget for the following year.

Constructing a Budget

Most school districts use GAAP (Generally Accepted Accounting Principles) in developing budgets. Even if you are not told what your account numbers are, the district is most likely following this plan. Try to get a copy of the chart of accounts. Although it is a confusing document covering all aspects of the educational program, check the budget lines you use for a better sense of what is included. With practice and experience you can learn to develop some wiggle room.

The simplest way to approach the budget process is to repeat and modify what was done in budgets of previous years (which is another reason to have a copy of the current budget). In the GAAP model, a budget line comprises six areas. The first is for the *fund* (most often yours are in 11—"general current expense"); the second is the *program* (which groups by grade level, special education, etc.); the third is *function* (100 is for instruction—and you are likely to fall under 200 for "support"). The fourth is *object*, and 610, "general supplies," is used for the bulk of your budget, as it includes books, periodicals, small equipment (items costing less than $2,000 or whatever the amount set as a "capital outlay"), and supplies. The last two numbers are for school and department.

The *object* called "purchased professional and technical supplies" (300) includes licensing for library automation systems and maintenance contracts (copiers, security systems, etc.). You might have other accounts as well for attending professional development workshops, or one for repairs.

Before you begin working on your budget, find out if there are any specific directions you must follow and worksheets you must use. There is considerable disparity among districts here. Ask about guidelines. You may be told that you must cut a percentage from what you received for this year because the district is on an austerity budget, or you may be given the percentage by which you are allowed to increase over the previous year. Note what your total will be and apply the percentage to the different sections of your budget. You may make shifts as you look at what you really need to buy, but this will get you started.

Although most of your purchases are lumped in one area, you usually need to show what you are requesting for the books, magazines, and so on. In a few localities, SLMSs are expected to list specific supplies they want. If you are faced with this, see if you can use general categories such as "repair and preservation materials" (glue, tape, etc.), because your exact needs will change by the time you have to prepare the POs.

To estimate costs for maintenance contracts and small equipment, call your vendors. They are accustomed to SLMSs anticipating price increases. With equipment, be sure to include costs for shipping and handling.

Districts typically ask why you want to acquire the items in your budget. If this is the case in your school, you will have to indicate the rationale for everything you list. Most often this is a very brief statement, and you can copy from what was done in previous years. Review these to see if they indicate a need connected to students. If not, revise them. For example, the reason for purchasing new books is *not* "to keep the collection current"; it is "to maintain standards for student research."

Special Projects

If budgets are based on what you received the previous year, how do you ever get to do anything new? Find out if your district has a procedure for special projects. This can be a one-time infusion of money or the first time an item must be included within the budget. An example of the former might be to acquire resources to meet the needs of a newly introduced course or to replace outdated books in some section of the collection. In the latter instance, it can cover costs associated with having added a number of new printers and copiers, or providing new electronic databases because too few are available to students.

Ask the school secretary for a copy of paperwork submitted for other special projects funded in the past. While you prefer something requested for the LMC, anything will help. Use what you are given as a guideline, and check your work with your principal or supervisor before submitting it so you have time to make revisions. To justify your proposal, refer back to your goal and vision and show how the project will improve student achievement. In many places today, nothing is funded if it does not address this issue.

A side benefit of a special project is that in some districts, when the project is approved, the money becomes a permanent part of your account. When you prepare your next budget, the funds for the project are now part of the base to which you add or delete the prescribed percentage.

FINDING ALTERNATIVE FUNDING

As noted in the opening of the previous section, budgets are limited, and you may want to find money in other places. Possible solutions range from the very ordinary to the complex. All require planning and a knowledge of procedures.

Birthday Clubs and Book Fairs

Elementary school SLMSs sometimes have a birthday club. Parents and others donate money for a book or books to honor the event. A bookplate with the child's name, occasion, and date is placed inside the purchased title. The child is usually the first to borrow it. Enterprising middle and high school SLMSs can modify the idea by seeing if parents would like to do the same thing to honor their child's admission into an honor society, winning an award, and so on. Be sure you are the one to choose the title, although you can present the donors with a list of possibilities or have a cart of previously purchased new books from which parents may choose, giving you a set amount of money as reimbursement. *A note of caution:* before you institute any such practice, check to be sure what guidelines exist for accepting gifts. These vary among districts, and in some places the school board may be the party that officially accepts them.

Book fairs are another potential source of funds. Either you or the parents' organization contracts with a company that provides the books, "wish list" forms, and other relevant items. Classes are scheduled first to browse and then to buy books offered at the fair, and parents are also invited. Although the fair is probably held in the LMC, the parents' organization frequently runs it and keeps all the profits. If that is the situation in your school, see if you can convince the executive board of the parents' group to give some of the profits from the fair to the SLMP. In other places, you may get a percentage of what was raised or some free books. Another scenario has you being the one in charge, with all the profits going to the LMC.

In all instances, you will need to plan. Will the LMC be closed or will there be limited access to it? What announcements of the fair are being sent out, and who is responsible for preparing them? Who is setting up the schedule for class visits to the book fair? How are you handling the students who have no money to buy anything? Who selects the titles—you or the vendor? Do you have a say in what is not appropriate? What is the procedure if popular books sell out? Who takes care of the money? To whom are checks made out? Who gets the volunteers needed to supervise the fair? Who trains them? Does the vendor bring in bookcases filled with the selections, or can you set up displays on tables where you can group titles to meet your students' needs and interests?

If your school does not have a book fair, you might want to begin one. Since you are originating the project, you will get to keep all the profits, although you will be working very hard on the days the fair is scheduled. It will be *your* responsibility to choose the books and steer parents and other visitors (in addition to classes) to appropriate titles. After securing permission to hold a fair, identify a vendor based on a company you met at a state conference, or by asking for recommendations on your state association's electronic discussion list or from other SLMSs in the district. Be sure to ask the parent organization for help during the days when the fair will occur. Provide that organization with the schedule so parents can volunteer for the times when their children are coming in.

Grants

Unless you have had previous experience with them, you probably should not try to obtain a large grant during your first year. A number of books are available on how to write the applications, and other titles list those grants geared to libraries. If and when you do decide to apply for one, start with these rather than investing heavy research time in locating potential grantors.

Many districts have a local education foundation. This is a far easier source of grant money and, depending on your location, can offer a substantial amount. Most do not want to replace but rather augment the budget process, so you are not likely to get money to hire a clerk from this source. However, some special project ideas can be funded this way. You might get a grant for an author visit, or to join with other SLMSs in the district to establish a core reference collection. If you want to inaugurate something new such as audiobooks or graphic novels, a grant will allow you to purchase enough titles to make an impact. The ideas are up to you. Again, tie your proposal to students.

Dollars and Sense

How many separate accounts do you have to prepare for your budget?

_____

Has the SLMP budget been increasing, holding steady, or decreasing? In the latter two instances, what justification can you make for a special project?

_____

Which of the suggested alternatives for funding are most likely to work for you this year? What do you have to do to put them in place?

_____

ACQUISITIONS

The purpose of a budget is to give you a source of funds from which to make purchases. The questions confronting you are rarely discussed in depth in library school, but your administrator will expect you to know what to do. How do you determine what to buy? How do you choose the right items? Where do you get them?

Although you should go through last year's POs when preparing your budget to be sure you include ongoing items such as licensing agreements, magazines and newspapers, and online databases, return to the POs as you begin to spend your money. Flag any that will be repeated so that you do not forget to order them.

Books

Technology notwithstanding, books are still central to an SLMP. Although you have probably located countless catalogs from assorted publishers, you will select most of your titles from journals such as *Booklist* and *School Library Journal*. (The authors' own publication, *The School Librarian's Workshop,* reviews over forty K–12 books in each issue.) At the elementary level, *The Horn Book* is another excellent source. As you go through these magazines, highlight the titles you want to add to your collection.

Have your secretary or a volunteer enter what you have checked off onto a spreadsheet or other running list of possible purchases. As noted in chapter 4, you will most likely be ordering these from a jobber. Most jobbers have a software program allowing you to simply enter a book's International Standard Book Number (ISBN)—the unique ten-digit or new thirteen-digit number that identifies the book and its format (trade, library binding, paperback, etc.). The price and other information will then come up. You can also insert a note so that you know in which magazine you saw the review, on what page, and whether it was starred.

Whether you are using a jobber's software or a spreadsheet, keep a running total of what you want to buy. If you do not know the net cost of the titles, figure a discount of 10 percent for library bound books, 35 percent for trade books, and nothing for reference and professional titles. Remember that you may have to add processing and shipping and handling costs. LMCs with security systems generally pay to have detection tags inserted, and many have paperbacks covered with hard plastic jackets. Automated LMCs also order bar codes put on books and electronic records which are uploaded into the catalog.

Call the jobber used by your predecessor and ask for a copy of the specifications to know how your books are prepared. While you will not revise these as yet, you should know what to expect. Although the cataloging and classification on most incoming titles are done, you will still have to review books when they arrive. Not only do you have to determine which ones belong in the reference collection, but you may also disagree with where something has been placed and need to change it.

If you do see vendors as recommended in chapter 8, you will also be acquiring titles through them. Go over the services they provide. As noted earlier, many will prepare the order for you to attach to the PO with a descriptive note that indicates the total is for the accompanying list of books. While vendors are not likely to cover dust jackets or insert security tags, they do catalog material and ship books with spine labels and book pockets. Data disks are generally available (which means everything is bar coded as well), but you will need to go over the records. These smaller dealers contract their cataloging, and some of it is not that good. You will have to decide whether poor or indifferent records are better than doing it in-house. (However, you might investigate companies such as Marcive—http://www.marcive.com—that will do quality work at a minimal cost to you.)

Reference books are often acquired directly from publishers. Although you buy fewer print encyclopedias than in the past, you should have two or three different sets, rotating purchases so that you have a new one about every other year. Vendors will probably see you about these, but if no one visits, check websites and find out how to buy the set you want. In middle and high schools, you will purchase a significant number of books from reference publishers such as ABC-CLIO, Gale, Marshall Cavendish, Salem, and Sharpe. Check your reference collection to become familiar with these companies and see how well you like their publications. They tend to create several formats and publish a number of titles that follow this pattern. If you like the way one treats a subject, you will probably like the remainder (if they are on topics covered in the school curriculum). Look for their catalogs and consider purchasing new titles that meet student and teacher needs in various subjects.

As you go through different avenues for selecting books, keep your goals in mind. Even the most generous budgets (and there are few out there) will not permit you to purchase all favorably reviewed titles. At first you will not be sure which departments or grade levels in your school make the greatest use of the LMC, so focus on creating a balance. Recognize that whatever age range you serve, some students will be reading above it and others below it.

Give a high priority to starred reviews, but do not think you must purchase all of them. If they do not fit your needs, do not buy them. Check to be sure you have recent award winners. Jobbers have lists of them, as do the various ALA divisions that select national winners. Depending on the grades you work with, you will be most interested in Caldecott and Newbery titles (see http://www.ala.org/alsc/), which are usually in the language arts curriculum, or the Michael L. Printz Award (see http://www.ala.org/yalsa/), but there are others as well. Scroll down to see what the different ALA divisions do by clicking on "Awards and Scholarships." Check to see if your state has a book award and be sure to get copies of those titles as well.

Online Databases and Periodicals

Review the databases to which the LMC subscribes. Locate the POs for them and find out when the subscriptions expire. Evaluate the databases' relevance to the curriculum and your goals during the year. If you have not been able to monitor the use of these resources, ask the vendors if they have a program you can access to do so. (Your technology department may have to set it up for you, as some lock down online subscriptions.)

Lack of use does not necessarily mean a database should be discontinued. Googling students often ignore what you have available. If you think a resource is valuable, plan to incorporate it into your instruction and share it with teachers to get them to require its use in upcoming assignments. If students remain resistant, or if you find few curriculum connections, consider dropping it.

Most of your magazines, as covered in chapter 4, are ordered through a periodical jobber. While these have ISSNs (International Standard Serial Numbers), you are unlikely to use them. Find the file—card or digital—that lists the individual titles to which you subscribe. You must keep track of issues as they arrive to ensure that you are not missing any. Your clerk or a volunteer can handle this. Rather than putting in a check mark, have them record the date. Each periodical has a different time when it arrives, some a full month before publication date, others relatively close to it. Unless you know the pattern, you will not realize that an issue is late. If too much time elapses before you file a request with your jobber (or the company if the title is one you order direct), it may not be replaceable. (Always check your school's main office before alerting your vendor to a missing issue. Secretaries and other staff members sometimes "borrow" a magazine from the incoming mail.)

The advent of full-text online databases has sharply cut the number of print magazines you must purchase. Students prefer online material, so if a magazine is only used for research purposes, you need not get the hard copy. Watch what students read when they have free time. One of the easiest ways is to see the magazines they leave lying around on tables. These are the titles you must continue to order. You can also have students recommend others that they feel should be part of the collection. Always consider to what extent these purchases will advance your goals. In other words, how do they fit into the larger picture?

Consortia

To take advantage of economies of scale, most locations have one or more consortia which you can join or to which you automatically belong. In addition to the reduced pricing they offer, check to see what other services they provide. Some give training on their databases or on other computer applications.

Explore their websites and contact the persons who can give you background and insight as to how the consortium can best meet your needs. Knowing what consortia can do for you and your teachers will be an aid to your planning.

Shifting Funds

One of the rarely discussed options is the ability to move funds between accounts. Even when you are very experienced with your school and budget process, it is sometimes difficult to project exactly what you will need for the following school year. Other than using one of the alternative sources of funding, you cannot get more money, but you can frequently shift funds from one account to another or within accounts.

For example, in the middle of the school year you might find you need a new online database. You may have put these resources under the GAAP's line for "purchased professional and technical services" and completely used up this account (which can be a good way to protect your budget, since administrators are loath to cut from this line while they dip freely into the tempting block of money in "library supplies"). If money is available from your book or supply purchases, you can submit a form to move it from one budget line to another, including a justification for your request. Have the school secretary explain the process to you.

Technically, anything in the same budget line does not need to be formally moved. So if you are using GAAP and need more money for books and have not as yet purchased a small piece of equipment, you are not legally required to request a transfer of funds. However, your district may still want you to file for the change.

Although funds can be moved from one account to another, there is one impenetrable wall. You cannot move money from a capital account to an instructional one. In the GAAP system, numbers beginning with 12 denote capital accounts, while those beginning with 11 indicate instructional accounts.

Buying Power

Which reviewing journals are you receiving? Do you need others?

_____

Who is your book jobber? Who is your periodical jobber?

_____

Which magazines do you think can be dropped? Are there any you wish to add?

_____

To which consortium do you belong? Is there one you should be joining?

_____

COLLECTION MAPPING

Not to be confused with curriculum mapping, collection mapping allows you to see how many books you have in a given section and how old they are. The planning purposes are obvious. You get to see where there are gaps that need to be filled and which areas are most in need of weeding. In the past, the process was tedious. You chose a Dewey Decimal range (or a special collection), pulled every tenth title within it, and noted its copyright date. Statistically, you came up with a relatively accurate assessment of your collection, but it was labor-intensive and very time-consuming even if volunteers did the work.

For those with an automated system, technology has reduced the process to a matter of minutes. Follett Library Resources offers TitleWise on its website (http://www.flr.follett.com), which will do it all for you and give you an eighteen-page printout. On your first visit to the website you will have to create an account, but you are under no obligation to buy anything. It takes a bit of time to enter your profile, since you need to determine what is to be included and how you want materials counted. For example, do you want your reference books analyzed separately or as part of their Dewey Decimal number? (Most likely you will prefer the former.) You can complete the profile at one time and do the mapping at another. Directions for uploading the information from your electronic records are fairly straightforward, but if you have difficulty, Follett's technical support staff will help.

Understanding the Data

Unless your collection is quite new, you will probably be surprised by the results. After the cover page, TitleWise gives you an overview of the analysis complete with the date it was done, automation system, total records (and the number of recognized call numbers—you should have over 95 percent identifiable), average age of titles, enrollment total, and number of books per student.

The next page gives the age, number, and percentage of the collection by Dewey Decimal 100s and other categories you have specified. Colorful bar and pie graphs follow to illustrate the information. Additional pages do the same breakdown by the 10s. The next analysis compares the percentage of holdings in a category with what Follett thinks it should be, giving you the differential, and does the same for the balance recommended in H. W. Wilson publications (e.g., *Books for the Senior High School*). Bar graphs are given for these as well. A list of totals by decade of copyright date with a bar graph is another eye-opener.

Next is "Age Sensitivity," which suggests the acceptable age for areas that date rapidly and the percentage of the collection which falls outside it. Follett sets this at five years (except for "Systems Data/Computer Programs," which become dated after only three years). Do not overreact to seeing that more than 90 percent of your titles are considered outdated. You *do* have a problem, but generally only the newest LMCs have very low percentages even in these "age-sensitive" areas.

Take time to look at what the numbers really mean. What stands out the most? Is the collection seriously unbalanced? Perhaps a previous SLMS had an interest in a subject and ordered far too many titles in that area, or you might be a magnet school with a focused curriculum. Are you lacking coverage on a topic that is an important part of the curriculum? Are your holdings seriously out of date? If your school has been around for some time, you will likely find that the average age of the collection is somewhere in the 1970s. Realize that in some areas, acceptable age varies among subjects. Art books have a much longer shelf life than science titles.

While you will not achieve Follett's recommendations, you will want to do what is possible to make the collection more current. Prepare a one- or two-page executive summary of the analysis, explaining the data and highlighting key areas that you wish to address. Send it to your principal and request a meeting to discuss it further. The report from Follett is so well done that it usually makes a tremendous impact. Talk about the possibility of a special project to fund acquisitions in areas you have identified. Find out if the principal would like you to send a copy of the collection analysis to the superintendent to support your request.

Weeding

After the collection mapping is completed, you have a guide as to where to begin weeding. If everything is very old, decide where to focus first. The most time-sensitive areas should be a priority, as well as subjects frequently researched by students. They have a predisposition to use the Internet for all their information needs. You will never convince them to turn to print resources if titles are outdated or even have an old-looking format.

Balance getting rid of what is old with eliminating too much of the collection. Remember that age is not the only determining factor. Some titles remain relevant even after many years. For example, despite the importance of currency in books on space travel, Willy Ley's *Rockets, Missiles, and Space Travel* published in 1957 is a classic showing what was advanced thinking in its day and should not be discarded if it is in reasonable shape. If you are unsure, check the various resources that list titles belonging in a collection for the grades you serve, such as works from H. W. Wilson mentioned earlier, *The Elementary School Library Collection* (Brodart), and *Best Books* (for different grade ranges) by John T. Gillespie and Catherine Barr (Libraries Unlimited).

Inform your principal that you are about to begin a weeding project. Explain how you plan to manage it and your purpose (tied to your goals and vision) for undertaking it. A few administrators do not want you to discard much, fearing you will go below the number of recommended books per student (given at twenty before electronic resources came into being). The results of your collection mapping should minimize this reaction.

Even if you have support for your plan, you need to find out what if any legal restrictions exist on tossing out discarded books. Some districts allow you to donate them (but some of what you are discarding should not be used by anyone) or let students and staff pick what they like. In other locations, how to dispose of materials bought with tax dollars is carefully circumscribed. Do not toss anything into trash barrels without ripping off covers. Although it may be personally abhorrent to do so, you do not want parents complaining that they bought books from the LMC at a local flea market or tag sale.

About the Books

What would you estimate is the average age of the books in your collection?

_____

Which areas do you think are most in need of weeding?

_____

Did collection mapping validate your guesses, or were you surprised?

_____

What is your highest achievable priority—weeding or filling in gaps?

_____

MANAGING YOUR SUPPORT STAFF

Whether you have a paid staff or volunteers, you are responsible for delegating and overseeing their work. A good rule of thumb is to treat paid staff like volunteers and volunteers as though they were on your staff. That is, address a clerk as if she were not an employee and could leave at any time, and show your volunteers that they have the same worth and merit as those being paid.

When you are new to a school, even if you have had experience elsewhere, support staff can make your life easier or more difficult. An excellent beginning is to ask what job they like best. The answers from your staff will alert you to the tasks you do not want to change for quite a while. Since volunteers do not show up every day, you cannot guarantee that they will always be assigned what they prefer, but try to have them do what they enjoy as often as possible.

Take some time to discover what the support staff's personal interests and talents are. Often you can make use of a particular ability. Someone may be a whiz at computer design and can help give a professional look to brochures and fliers you prepare. Someone else might love detail work and be great at inputting data, such as entering the information on books you want to purchase. You will not only get valuable assistance but also have committed helpers because they are doing what they love and feel validated.

Planning will help you make the best use of support staff. Keep track of who knows how to do which jobs. With volunteers, list them all down one column and put the different tasks along the top. Put a check under each one they have been trained to do. Many people are unaware of how to put books in Dewey Decimal sequence. Others may not realize that when shelves are straightened (usually after "reading" them to see that they are in order), the spines are brought to the edge of the shelf, using the heel of the hand to align them.

Have experienced volunteers demonstrate their understanding of how the various tasks are accomplished so that you learn what past practices have been. For example, how do they process books? If you need to correct someone, do so carefully, suggesting that you want everyone using the same procedures, and then have these helpers train others.

Prepare a list of tasks you want to get done for the week and have volunteers initial the ones they complete. Make another list of the ranges of call numbers on a row of bookcases; for example, FIC A to FIC G, or 520 A to 549 S. These should represent a logical beginning and ending point. Assign one or more ranges to each volunteer. When they have read the shelves, have them put their initials on the sheet along with the date. This way you can be sure the collection is kept in reasonable order.

Volunteers are more productive and committed if they feel responsible for a piece of the SLMP. You might give someone who loves detail and working with her hands the job of repairing books. Another might check in and display current magazines, while someone else files older copies in the back. When a task requires particular supplies—glue, paste, scissors, and so on—make a "task box" with all the materials inside, putting the job and the volunteer's name on the outside. If they need it, give them shelf space in your back room to store what they are working on.

If you are lucky enough to have paid staff, let them know you are grateful to have them show you the ropes. Ask how they like to be managed. Do they want you to give them daily tasks, or would they rather have you let them know what needs to get done and what your priorities are? Will they be comfortable with you checking every so often, or do they prefer you to go over the work at the end? Do whatever you can to accommodate them.

Whether you have paid or volunteer staff, keeping track of what everyone is doing and making sure that nothing slips through the cracks is a delicate balance of trusting and inspecting. You must see that tasks are properly accomplished without being critical. If something is not done to your standards, avoid making the person feel wrong.

As you review what happened, use "I" statements rather than ones with the word "you" in them, and try to avoid negatives. For example, "I know there are a lot of steps to getting a book repaired and back on the shelf, so it is easy to skip something. I found a number of them on the book cart without bar codes. What do you need to help you keep track of everything that must be done?" By allowing those who made the error to participate in finding a solution, you will empower them rather than having them become defensive and argumentative, and—in the case of volunteers—having them quit.

Sometimes the most important planning you do is thinking before you speak.

Supporting Support Staff

What tasks are done by your support staff?

_____

What can you do to acknowledge their work or validate their contributions?

_____

How well does your management style mesh with how your support staff wants to be managed?

_____

Key Ideas

- All projects require planning.
- Planning begins with a vision.
- Goals should further your vision.
- Action steps help you accomplish your goals.
- For a large project, gather as much information as you can relating to it and keep everything together.
- Avoid becoming overwhelmed by using microscoping, periscoping, and telescoping.
- Share plans with your support staff.
- Budgets are based on past budgets.
- Learn as much as you can about how the budget cycle and process works.
- Identify other funding avenues to subsidize projects.
- Use reviewing journals as your primary source for selecting books.
- Request a copy of your specifications from your jobber.
- Determine whether you need hard copies of all the magazines to which you subscribe.
- Become familiar with the services of any consortia to which you belong.
- Collection mapping suggests areas for weeding and new acquisitions.
- Collection mapping is an aid to planning and demonstrating needs to administrators.
- Know what tasks your support staff can accomplish and look for their special skills.
- Always show respect to your support staff.

NOTE

1. American Association of School Librarians, Association for Educational Communications and Technology, *Information Power: Building Partnerships for Learning* (Chicago: American Library Association, 1998), 4.

CHAPTER 10

Technology and You

And now for a game of owl and mouse.

*T*his is the one chapter you probably think you do not need. Those fresh out of library school have had courses on web design and presentation media, among others. If you have just changed districts or buildings, technology has been an integral part of your job. While you are comfortable using it, there are a number of other aspects involved in becoming familiar with what technology you have, helping teachers integrate it into the curriculum, and, most important of all, developing a good relationship with the technology department.

Those with whom you will need to develop a relationship vary widely from place to place. In large districts there may be staff assigned to specific buildings. The most common situation is having tech people go where needed (according to their priorities—not necessarily yours), and some of you will find that there is only one person to cover everything. There are districts without *any* tech staff, although this is becoming rarer. The job falls to an assortment of people which most often includes you and other tech-savvy teachers. For big jobs, the administration contracts with an outside networking company.

YOU AND THE TECHNOLOGY DEPARTMENT

Although teachers generally pay little attention to the people in the technology department (except when things go wrong), you need to get to know almost all of them. Try to meet with the head of the department as soon as possible. Ask for a copy of the district's technology plan, and have the department head explain what he thinks are its chief points and main direction. This is *not* the time to disagree with anything that is there.

Note whether a school library media specialist is on the technology committee, and if there is no representation, ask to be appointed. Let the technology coordinator (or whoever chairs the committee) see that you are interested and technologically competent. You do not want to appear to be judging or criticizing his decisions. Show that your area of expertise complements but does not compete with his.

In the course of your discussion, try to discover what the technology department hates to do. Perhaps they find setting up teachers' accounts a drag on their time, or they dislike loading new student information into your library automation system database because they have so many other responsibilities. Perhaps they are responsible for all the schools' web pages and find it a nuisance. If any of those tasks make the library media program run more smoothly or can be a bridge to promoting your relations with the faculty, offer to handle them yourself.

If you are seen as a willing partner rather than one more complainer, the tech people will go out of their way to help you when you need it. You may find them reluctant to give you too many "rights," but do not take it personally. Their first responsibility is to maintain the integrity of the network. While you may feel they lock it down too tightly, they fear student hackers with too much time on their hands or careless teachers who let viruses slip through e-mails despite warnings and alerts.

During your initial meeting, get the names, responsibilities, e-mail addresses, and phone extensions of everyone in the department. Consider inviting them to the library media center and offer snacks as a way of getting to know them all. Make sure that your first communications with them are *not* about problems. Think of some questions that you would like them to answer about hardware, software, or procedures.

Get a sense of where their biases are. Do they prefer PCs or Macs? Are they committed to Microsoft or are they advocates of open source, a free, web-based platform using Linux? If you find that you do not agree with what they see as the right or sole choices, avoid direct confrontation. Slowly push for a more inclusive approach, but do not criticize their views.

Be sure you know the procedures for reporting problems and requesting assistance. When you have developed the relationship, you might be able to go outside these steps in an emergency. For the moment, strictly adhere to the established process.

Tech Talk

Where is the technology department based?

_____

Is there a tech person assigned to your school?

_____

What tasks do you think you can take on to assist the technology department and make your school library media program more efficient?

_____

FILTERS AND INTELLECTUAL FREEDOM

Almost all school districts have filters to prevent students from accessing inappropriate Internet sites. This is done mostly to comply with e-rate regulations that give schools a steep discount for telecommunication services. In addition, school boards fear lawsuits from parents whose children may have inadvertently or purposely been exposed to pornographic web pages.

Filters invariably come into conflict with the ALA Code of Ethics and "Access to Resources and Services in the School Library Media Program" (see chapter 11), since both of these documents promote open access to information. As students are inevitably blocked from legitimate websites, you may find you have difficulty reconciling your philosophy with these infringements on intellectual freedom. Since you are new, you will have to respond cautiously, but that does not mean you should abdicate your principles.

Find out the procedure for having a site opened. Be sure to have any required forms at hand so you can request that it be unblocked as rapidly as possible. Anticipate potential problems. If you know what a class will be researching, perform searches in advance of their visit and inform the technology department (or whatever the process is) of the valid, informative web pages that students will need to access. Once the pages have been opened, prepare a list of them so the class knows they are available. A side benefit of this is that once teachers know that you are performing this service, they will give you more advance notice of their plans.

Keep track of search terms that cause the filter to intervene and the sites students are prevented from seeing. When you have a reasonable number of them, perhaps noting a pattern, ask for another meeting with the head of the technology department. Show him what you have collected and find out if there are categories that can be unblocked (particularly if you are in a high school) so that there are not so many individual requests.

Eventually, you might explore the possibility of finding another filter with the cooperation and support of the technology department. You want one that will give you maximum control. Filters vary, and some have restrictions that cannot ever be overridden.

Once you have earned the trust of the department and administrators, see if you can be given the authority to open sites. Correlate this with your responsibility for book selection. As part of your professional expertise, you know what material is age-appropriate. This is as true for

Internet sites as it is for books. Certainly, there are titles that you would never purchase for the students you serve. Selection is not censorship, but filters most often are.

Filtering Freedom of Access

What filter is being used in the district? Explore the company's website to find out more about it.

_____

What is the procedure for opening blocked websites? Who has the authority to do so?

_____

Perform searches on curriculum-related topics. How often does the filter block access?

_____

ACCEPTABLE USE POLICIES IN ACTION

Chapter 4 discussed acceptable use policies as something to look for when getting yourself organized, but you need to pay more attention to them once you have settled into your new position. If you collect the signed statements from students (and sometimes staff) agreeing to abide by the policy, this process is another link between you and the technology department. Know which of you is responsible for what part of the AUP process and keep the lines of communication open.

For example, who keeps the signed forms? If you maintain the file, are you the one who allows those who have turned in their statements access to the network? Even if you are not, you can expect to have to walk them through the initial logging-on steps. Violating the AUP often carries a penalty of being blocked from the network for a period of time. Who handles this?

You might want to check how often penalties have been imposed. Although the AUP discusses consequences for breaking the rules, unless there has been harm to the system, districts often let students off with a warning. The reasons for doing so may range from the difficulty in proving willful disobedience or the negative academic effect of barring a student from computer access. Having a sense of how stringently the AUP is enforced will guide you in your response if you see a violation.

Find out when the acceptable use policy was instituted. School districts have a habit of establishing policies and never revisiting them. Given rapid changes in technology, this is one document that should be reviewed at least biennially. First see whether all important components are included in the policy, such as a statement about complying with copyright law while on the Internet. The Virginia Department of Education (http://www.pen.k12.va.us/VDOE/Technology/AUP/home .shtml) offers an excellent list of AUPs, as does Education World (http://www.educationworld.com/a_curr/curr093.shtml). If any sections are missing from the AUP, share what you have found with the technology department to see what the next steps might be.

If the AUP is several years old, it will not reflect newer technological issues schools are facing. Rather than have the AUP just cover computer use, it might be a good idea for the policy to incorporate the acceptable use of all telecommunication devices as well. For example, students who text message each other the answers to tests have become an issue in many locations. Blogs which may be used for bullying or attacking teachers or putting students at risk are another issue. How are podcasts handled? These concerns are not yet included in most AUPs but are worth discussing, so that a revised document can encompass all aspects of technology affecting schools today.

Acceptable and Unacceptable Access

What are your responsibilities for the AUP?

_____

When was the AUP last updated?

_____

Are penalties reasonable in your opinion? Too harsh? Too lenient?

_____

What areas of technology are not covered by the AUP?

_____

ONLINE DATABASES

Previous discussions of online databases in chapters 4 and 9 looked at which ones you own and how to go about continuing them or ordering new ones. However, you should also be reviewing them in other ways. Each database provides "administrative" access that allows you to control different aspects such as opening screens or learning how often it has been accessed within a given time frame. While you will not be doing this often, you should be sure you have the rights to view this part of the database and make changes.

Plan to explore one online database each week. Although this means taking an hour or two after school, it is well worth your time. In addition to trying a typical student search and seeing how results are displayed, check other resources of the database. When would it be advisable for students to use the advanced search (they almost never do)? Are tutorials available, and who would most benefit from them—you, teachers, or students? How many subject areas or courses would find helpful information on this database?

As you work your way through the databases, develop a list of their resources for each department. Everyone can use a general encyclopedia; a periodical database is also applicable to most subject areas. Subject-specific databases can sometimes be broader than expected. For example, a literature database might be used at times with history or even some science courses. Distribute the list to teachers—and your administrator.

If you have identified subjects that are not properly covered in the databases, ask for volunteers to help you explore possibilities to add to your holdings. Having teachers involved in the process not only builds support, but also gives you an opportunity to show them how to incorporate these resources into their classes. Even before the new databases are purchased, you are likely to have those same teachers set up research projects with you.

In chapter 6, we recommended steps for showing teachers that a particular database might be helpful for a current project. If you are to get value for the amount of money you spend on these resources, you must build support for them. Students will not seek out databases on their own. They invariably will start with Google unless directed otherwise. Even with strong recommendations from you, only a few will follow your advice.

The only way to get students to access online databases with any frequency is to have teachers require them as one or more sources for a project. Since you now have a thorough understanding of what each database contains, you can gently make your case for them. Among the reasons to present are the credibility and authority of these resources, as well as their importance in preparing students for college.

Electronic Reference

How many online databases do you own?

_____

Which subject areas have the most electronic resources? Which have the least?

_____

How often do you use these resources when working with students?

_____

Which databases, if any, do students seem to like? Why?

_____

LIBRARY MANAGEMENT SYSTEMS

Whatever your preference for an automation system, unless your school does not have one, you are stuck with what you have for a while. As with much that happens in the LMC, you are expected to know all about how to run this program whether or not you have ever used it before. In addition, despite the presence of companies that have been around for some time, there is much more instability than you might think, and you need to be prepared for change.

Your System

Although you know how to create a MARC record necessary for an automated library, you are not likely to be familiar with all the different library management systems. Follett is the biggest vendor for the school market, but numerous other players are out there. When starting in a new job, you are probably unfamiliar with the system you have, yet you will need to be up and running with it as soon as school begins.

First you must see if you can log in to the system. If not, immediately get in touch with the technology department. Locate any manuals and also check out the company's website. It probably will not take long to figure out the basics—checking books in and out and accessing the OPAC—but you need to manage other components quickly.

What is most important is to be sure that all incoming students (and new teachers) are loaded into the database. Who does this? If it is you, where do you get the data and how is it uploaded? For the latter question, you can call tech support. The first issue may take more time to discover. If you are not the one responsible for getting the data, who is and when does it occur?

Your next concern is entering records for new books into the system. See whether these are on a disk or come via the Internet. Next ask the vendor's help desk how to get them loaded. If a teacher needs a book before you have it shelf-ready, do not hesitate to check it out by making a paper notation of what was borrowed and by whom. Despite being harried and worried about all you have to learn, remember that service to faculty and students comes first. It is not the end of the world if you lose track of one book.

Once you have mastered these core operations, contact the vendor and see if the company can send a sales rep who can walk you through the system without charging for training. While this person usually cannot go through all the steps on how to generate various reports, at least she can show you what is available. Identify the reports you will need early and review how to generate them in the manual. You can always call for help as you try to produce your first one. Check to see if another SLMS in the district can go over the process with you as well.

An Eye to the Future

Over the past five years, as most library media centers have become automated, a feeling of complacency has settled over SLMSs. They learn their system and every few years expect the upgrades covered by the licensing agreement. A few bumps have shown up. Most companies charged a sizable fee when they switched from DOS to Windows, since it was more than an upgrade. While Mac-based systems did not have this specific problem, school districts using multiple platforms sometimes discovered that their automation program was not compatible with a higher version of a Mac operating system, or an upgrade did not work with the current Macs. In addition, many schools have paid to have their OPAC (and sometimes the entire system) on the Internet.

Unless you have been attending national library conferences and keeping an eye on which vendors are present and what they are offering, you may not have been aware of a larger problem. Companies are disappearing or are being bought out by others. Some established systems are not keeping pace with developments.

When a vendor goes out of business or is taken over by some other company, what happens to your management system? The answer is uncertain. The new owner may maintain it for a while, but is likely to expect you to migrate to something else at a considerable charge. In other cases, what was a state-of-the-art system when purchased may no longer be anywhere near that. Do you stay with an out-of-date product? What happens when a software upgrade will not run on the older equipment you have? Do you stay with the older version of the software? How long will it be supported?

While these are not concerns that should trouble you in the first months you are on the job, you need to be aware of what the future might bring. If and when the time comes to select a new library management system, you should have some options and a plan.

Learn how strong your vendor is and explore what else is out there. When districts first automated, the practice was to automate a few schools each year, distributing the costs over time. Now if you have to migrate, everyone must move at once, and, even with discounts for purchasing a number of site licenses, the price may still be prohibitive.

One growing possibility is to select an open source vendor. Instead of using a Microsoft operating system, these are based on Linux, which carries no underlying licensing fees. The product is completely web-based, and you have the option of hosting it yourself or having the company do so at a moderate charge. In either case, the program will run on almost any computer, reducing the pressure for newer equipment.

Some technology people are skeptical of the value of open source software, having invested a lot of time in training on Microsoft; others embrace it heartily. At middle and high school levels you will find your students quite knowledgeable about open source and strong advocates of using it. Indeed, most of them prefer Firefox to Internet Explorer as their web browser.

If your district has not yet automated, be sure to include open source systems in your RFP when you are ready. For the majority of you who are automated, depending on how secure you believe your system is, do a search and see what is out there. Although open source programs have been in successful operation for some time, not all of them have gone public as yet. More are appearing even as this is being written.

As you look at your options, make sure you are keeping all stakeholders informed. If others are going to be making the final decision as to which program you will be using, it is important that they are not only aware of your preferences but also *agree* with them. This may require a mini-marketing campaign on your part.

Managing Your System

If your LMC is automated, what system and version are you running? Is it the latest one?

_____

If you are unfamiliar with the system, how intuitive is it? Can you do basic operations on it?

_____

What have you learned by checking the vendor's website?

_____

ASSESSING HARDWARE AND SOFTWARE

If one does not exist, develop a spreadsheet listing all the equipment in the LMC. You need to know what you have and the approximate age and capacity of the computers. Is everything connected to the Internet? Can other computers in the school access the OPAC and online databases available in the LMC?

Do you have wireless laptops or a mobile computer lab which you are responsible for circulating? Are digital cameras and video equipment housed in the LMC? What about video projectors? In most schools, the SLMS manages all of this, does minor maintenance, responds when something malfunctions during a class (not a possibility if you are rigidly scheduled), and sends items needing serious repair either to the technology department or to a designated company. Be sure you know what you are expected to do, since this may not have been discussed during the hiring process.

Locate as many manuals as you can for your equipment and keep them in a file so that you can find them when something goes wrong. The technology department may be able to help with some of this. If you are unsure about operating one or more of these items, see if you can find a faculty member or someone from the technology department to give you a quick demonstration, then practice on your own. Do not worry about showing that you don't know how to do everything. There is so much technology and so many significant variations among models that no one knows it all.

See what software is running on the computers. In addition to word processing, you should have a spreadsheet and a presentation program. You most likely will not have a database program. If you feel the need for one, speak with the technology department. You will probably find that it is available but not loaded unless someone puts in a request for it. Also see if you have or can get Adobe Photoshop and Microsoft Publisher, since these will help you in making the displays and brochures that are part of your public relations or marketing campaigns.

Are there CD programs as well? How old are these? Should any be replaced? Where is the server located, and do you have any responsibility for it?

While some of these items are not critical in your first few months, you don't want to overlook their existence. Be aware of what you don't know and plan to fill in the blanks at a later date.

Nuts and Bolts

How many computers and printers are in the LMC?

_____

What other peripherals do you have?

_____

What are your responsibilities for circulating equipment?

_____

Key Ideas

■ Make yourself helpful to the technology department.

■ Filters are a fact of life, but you can work to mitigate their negative impact on students' access to information.

■ Know how you and the technology department maintain and enforce the AUP.

■ Review the AUP to see whether it includes current technology.

■ Explore the LMC's online databases thoroughly to be able to make maximum use of them.

■ Broaden the coverage of online databases so that all subject areas are represented.

■ Persuade teachers to require online databases as sources for research projects.

■ Get whatever passwords you need to access your library management system as soon as possible.

■ Try to have new students and teachers loaded into the database before school starts.

■ Use a combination of manuals, tech support, sales reps, and district SLMSs to get up to speed on the system.

■ Start investigating the field to prepare for a future migration to another system.

■ Inventory your hardware so you know what you have.

■ Request any software programs that you feel are necessary for the SLMP.

CHAPTER 11

Ethics, Standards, and You

I can stand firmly on these!

Professional Ethics
- Code of Ethics and Library Bill of Rights
- Intellectual Freedom
- Privacy

Information Literacy Standards
- *Information Power*
- National Educational Technology Standards for Students

Copyright and Plagiarism
- Fair Use
- Preventing Plagiarism

Subject Standards
- National Standards
- State Standards

No Child Left Behind

*K*nowing that you are upholding solidly established principles and requirements rather than operating from your own personal reactions gives what you do a higher level of credibility. Part of the firm foundation from which you operate includes the ethical standards common to all librarians no matter the area in which they work. In addition, you should be addressing national as well as state and local standards in your teaching. When the occasion arises, let people know that your decisions are rooted in your professionalism.

PROFESSIONAL ETHICS

The members of a profession embrace its ethics, and there are several such statements issued by the American Library Association with which you need to be familiar. They emphasize the commitment of librarians to championing intellectual freedom in all its manifestations. Some of these statements are obvious; others are more subtle. You may find the ALA's unswerving dedication to the concept of intellectual freedom to be daunting at times, but you need to recognize it as a core value of the profession.

Code of Ethics and Library Bill of Rights

Whether or not you covered them in your course work, be sure you have at least scanned the ALA Code of Ethics. Its history goes back to 1939, and the current statement was adopted in 1995. One of its more profound ideas is expressed in the introduction: "We are members of a profession explicitly committed to intellectual freedom and the freedom of access to information. We have a special obligation to ensure the free flow of information and ideas to present and future generations."[1] With that assertion, the ALA takes a stand for the profession as a staunch defender of the First Amendment.

The Code of Ethics is brief enough that it will not take long to read. You should feel a sense of pride at belonging to a profession that serves a vital function in a democracy which cannot exist without free-flowing ideas unfettered by censorship. In addition to its stand on intellectual freedom, the Code of Ethics upholds patrons' right to privacy and demands that coworkers and colleagues be treated well.

Furthermore, librarians are enjoined to separate their personal philosophies from that of their institution or professional association.

For example, you do not determine whether a book should or should not be purchased based on your own biases. You can be opposed to an author's point of view but still must add it to your collection if its presence provides the balance of opinions which each library must offer.

Along with the Code of Ethics, you should have the Library Bill of Rights and the document entitled "Access to Resources and Services in the School Library Media Program."[2] It is essential for you to know that while curriculum and grade levels are important factors in materials selection, you are expected to provide a broad range of ideas and information to "create and sustain an atmosphere of open inquiry."[3]

Intellectual Freedom

Although discussed in reference to administrative policies in chapter 4 and the presence of filters in chapter 10, intellectual freedom affects so many of your decisions as a school library media specialist that it requires a more thorough analysis. The *Intellectual Freedom Manual* from the ALA's Office for Intellectual Freedom should be on the shelf where you keep all your professional tools.[4] The Library Bill of Rights and its many associated statements with their interpretations and history are included in this book, along with the history behind the previously mentioned text "Access to Resources and Services in the School Library Media Program." The manual also explores the importance of protecting the freedom to read with additional policies and guidelines and their histories. Although the text "Free Access to Libraries for Minors" applies only in public library settings, as schools are governed by different laws, students do have rights as discussed in "Minors' First Amendment Rights to Access Information," which covers relevant Supreme Court decisions.[5] Particularly helpful is the appendix information on how to navigate the website of the Office for Intellectual Freedom.

In library school it was easy to accept the importance of upholding this fundamental right. But when you are alone in your library media center and wondering whether to buy a novel that explores a homosexual relationship, you may silently compromise your principles and philosophy to preserve your job. Sometimes you hold "questionable" books to a higher selection standard, perhaps purchasing one that has earned a starred review or won an award but not getting titles that were merely favorably assessed. You can rationalize this as book selection, but you know it really is self-censorship.

No one will be aware if you deny your students access to these resources, but you should be honest with yourself about your decision-making process. Certainly, you should be aware of community standards. If you are in a Bible Belt town and it is your first year on the job, adding books on witchcraft or with sexually explicit themes is likely to get you fired—unless you have a selection policy (see chapter 4) in place that defines the basis for acquisitions. Until you have the backing of a policy, you might proceed with some caution and build your reputation before choosing obvious red flag titles. But realize that in these conservative districts students have the least access to information about ideas that concern and trouble them. If the LMC and the public library choose not to purchase controversial books, where can these students go?

Remember the distinction between selection and censorship as explained in chapter 4. Selection looks at the item as whole, while censorship seeks to reject based on "snippets." The use of profanity when appropriate to the setting is no reason for not purchasing a title. However, if the theme of a book is centered on a sexual relationship, you might rightfully consider it unsuitable for fifth or sixth graders. This is professional judgment. Whatever you choose to do, you know the difference between selection and censorship.

Upholding professional ethics can be scary. For those with the courage and convictions to do so, remember you are not alone. The ALA and its Office for Intellectual Freedom, along with your state association's Intellectual Freedom Committee, will offer you advice and guidance if you are faced with a challenge. As you make decisions in this area, consider your philosophy and what it means to be a professional.

Privacy

Another aspect of intellectual freedom is the right to privacy. What someone chooses to read should not be made known to others. Although in some legal cases warrants have been issued to obtain patron borrowing records, the issue has had more national attention since the passage of the USA PATRIOT Act of 2001, and the ALA Council has passed resolutions concerning these new infringements on individual rights. Although the 2006 extension of the act removed some of the restrictions on secrecy involved when libraries are required to respond to federal demands for information, much of what the ALA and other organizations concerned with freedom of speech consider violations of rights are still in place. While it is unlikely that the FBI will be calling at your LMC, you should think about the records you keep. Most library management systems allow you to track what users have borrowed. While it might be nice to trace who were the last people to check out a book that has been damaged, it is far riskier to have that data available to those who might be searching for other information. Be sure that you have turned off the feature, so that no one is tempted to go on a fishing trip.

Many SLMSs send student overdue notices to homeroom teachers. As long as these are in envelopes with the recipients' names on the outside, you are preserving student privacy. However, if you send these as sheets of paper to be distributed, you are permitting others to know what individuals are reading.

States have different laws regarding what information parents can access. In general, they have a right to censor what their own children read (but not what others read) and usually are entitled to get that information—if it is available. They can also file a lawsuit if they think you have infringed on their child's privacy.

You and anyone who works in the LMC should be aware of national and state laws on privacy, as well as any local regulations. Another book for your professional shelf is *Privacy in the 21st Century: Issues for Public, School, and Academic Libraries*. Almost all of its chapters have information that affects schools. In particular, read the chapter that focuses on how the issue of privacy affects LMCs.[6]

Ethical Issues

What wording in the Code of Ethics or Library Bill of Rights is part of your philosophy?

_____

How would you characterize your district's attitude toward controversial topics?

_____

Does your collection have nonfiction titles dealing with these issues? Fiction titles?

_____

Where are you possibly violating students' rights to privacy?

_____

INFORMATION LITERACY STANDARDS

One of your primary responsibilities is to instill information literacy concepts in your students. Two sets of national standards detail what they should learn. The first is the jointly written guidelines from the ALA and the Association for Educational Communications and Technology.

The second is the National Educational Technology Standards for Students (NETS-S).

Information Power

In previous chapters we referred to the philosophy, mission, and vision for your program as they appear in *Information Power: Building Partnerships for Learning,* as well as this book's explanation of the roles you play in the educational community, but these were introductory concepts. When you prepare your lessons, you need to concentrate on the nine standards for information literacy as presented in *Information Power.* The first three standards describe how information-literate students seek information, the next three characterize the behaviors of independent learners, and the final three focus on students' ethical and social responsibility.[7]

Although you probably studied *Information Power* in library school, you need to look at it with fresh eyes. The examples of the standards in action and how they link to subject area standards will have much more meaning now that you are developing your school library media program. The ten principles for learning and teaching in chapter 4 are a guide for how to integrate the standards.[8] Chapter 5 deals with how you are to provide access to information and is firmly anchored in the profession's commitment to intellectual freedom.[9] Together these chapters are the framework for your SLMP.

National Educational Technology Standards for Students

In addition to *Information Power,* you should be familiar with NETS-S. Developed by the International Society for Technology in Education (ISTE), these standards identify six areas that form the "Technology Foundation Standards for Students" and can be downloaded for free from the ISTE website.[10] Performance indicators suggest what is appropriate for different grade ranges. Since most states have adopted these standards, you will want to incorporate them into your teaching. Check the site for lesson plans.

The NETS project also has standards for teachers and administrators. Review these with your principal and determine how you can contribute by presenting workshops that incorporate the standards for the faculty. It might even be helpful for you to have an individual session with your administrator. Consider purchasing some of the resources for your professional collection, and alert the staff once you have cataloged the material.

National Standards

To what extent are you able to accomplish the first of the learning and teaching principles in *Information Power*?

Is your school meeting the "essential conditions" critical to creating an environment that permits the "powerful use of technology" as identified in the NETS-S section of the ISTE website?

Where do you see an overlap between *Information Power*'s Information Literacy Standards and NETS-S?

COPYRIGHT AND PLAGIARISM

Violations of copyright and plagiarism are endemic in today's electronic environment. Teachers have regularly assumed "fair use" for many infringements of the copyright law. Students had been plagiarizing well before the advent of word processing and the Internet, but technology has made this so easy that it now exists on a scale unthinkable in the past. The ethical use of material is part of the Information Literacy Standards, so it is incumbent on you to bring this knowledge to everyone in the school.

Fair Use

One of your more uncomfortable tasks is to alert teachers to when they are improperly copying print material or using videos in their classes. The problem is that the law on fair use is a quagmire; for many instances there are guidelines, but these are subject to revision if a court takes a different stance. Most often the issue revolves around whether or not the four factors for fair use have been met. The law applies differently to students and teachers, and both need to have some understanding of it. Be prepared to explain what is and is not legal when using motion picture clips and other digital media within a presentation.

Be sure to have a sign about illegal copying posted next to every photocopier. You are required to have it. Purchase as many of these signs as you need from library supply houses. (Remind other departments and areas that have photocopiers that they must also display this statement.)

Another necessary addition for your professional shelf is *Copyright Law for Librarians and Educators: Creative Strategies and Practical Solutions*, by Kenneth Crews (Chicago: American Library Association, 2005). Note that the Digital Millennium Copyright Act of 1998 amended the law giving copyright holders more rights.

In addition to the book by Crews, you can also search the ALA website for a wealth of information on the topic of copyright law. The University of Maryland University College has a comprehensive, easy-to-understand website at http://www.umuc.edu/library/copy.html# whatis.[11] For further help, go to http://www.copyright.gov. You can attend copyright workshops at national or state conferences to keep up with the most current interpretations of the law.

Preventing Plagiarism

Two types of plagiarism typically occur in schools. The first is the deliberate submission of work done by someone else. The second is improperly quoting from sources. In the former case, students who are overburdened or just not ethical enough to care obtain a paper and turn it in as their own. The Internet is filled with sites that offer these papers for free or a fee. Some go so far as to indicate the typical grade that can be expected, so that a D student does not turn in an A paper and raise red flags. Their availability is so widespread that some sites specialize in popular topics such as Fitzgerald or Hemingway.

To reduce the amount of willful plagiarism, you need to first raise teachers' awareness of the extent of the problem. While some teachers are familiar with the most popular sites offering research papers, such as http://www.schoolsucks.com, there are a host of others, including the ironically named http://www.non-plagiarized-termpapers.com. Send teachers a list of such websites, which you can easily obtain by doing an online search.

Next, discuss three methods for dealing with the problem. Begin with education. Students need to know that plagiarism is a violation of school policy and that there are penalties that will be imposed for it. Let them know that plagiarism's repercussions are more severe in college, where it can lead to dismissal from the school. Oddly, many students do not realize that you can get penalized beyond having to redo the paper.

The second method is probably the most difficult one. Teachers need to redesign their research projects to make plagiarism more difficult. (Helping them make these changes can prove to be an excellent way to promote collaboration.) In addition to requiring a number of interim steps which *must* be completed before the final paper is accepted, such as an annotated bibliography, working outline, essential questions, and note cards, the topics themselves should be modified so that students are forced to reflect on the information they have found. Having them make oral presentations with questions from the teacher and class also inhibits plagiarizing.

A final method is to purchase a software product such as Turnitin .com which can be used to check for online plagiarism. A number of colleges and schools use it, but the system is not perfect and should not be the only defense against the practice. In addition to knowing their students' writing styles, teachers (with your help) need to take a close look at the "works cited" page of students' papers. Journals not available on online databases and invented titles are some of the red flags. If the books cited are not in your catalog or the public library's, require the student to show where the information was obtained.

Inadvertent plagiarism has also become a serious problem since cutting and pasting became available with word processing programs. Students need to realize that just changing one or two words in a sentence from a source does not constitute paraphrasing. Early in the term paper project, either you or the teacher should present a lesson on how to restate something. Again, requiring note cards can help forestall the problem.

A search on avoiding plagiarism will turn up a number of college websites with excellent information on the topic. Share these with your teachers and give students helpful handouts from these sites. Be sure to cite them appropriately.

Intellectual Property

What aspects of fair use are most likely to be violated by teachers? By students?

_____

What copyright resources do you have on hand? What do you still need?

_____

How do you plan to begin discussing the plagiarism issue with teachers?

_____

Which websites will you use for information on avoiding plagiarism?

_____

SUBJECT STANDARDS

Education today is standards- and test-driven. School budgets in many places fund only those departments or activities that result in student achievement. While a host of research studies demonstrate that an active SLMP promotes such achievement, you must also show that you contribute to helping students attain the required standards. Whether you collaborate with teachers or, because of a rigid schedule, work alone with students, your instruction should connect to national and state standards in the various subject areas as well as those for information literacy.

National Standards

One of the best websites for educators, Education World (http://www .educationworld.com/standards/#states), has the national standards for fine arts, language arts (including foreign languages), mathematics, physical education and health, science, and social studies. These standards link to NETS-S for technology and to the ALA for the nine Information Literacy Standards with indicators. Most of the standards are subdivided by grade level, with specific benchmarks that students are expected to achieve. Language arts, for example, has twelve integrated standards for all grades, and foreign language standards are divided into five areas for K–12 students. For more details on these two, you will need to purchase *Standards for the English Language Arts* from the National Council of Teachers of English (http://www.ncte.org/ about/over/standards) and *Foreign Language Standards: Linking Research, Theories, and Practices* from the American Council on the Teaching of Foreign Languages (http://www.actfl.org/i4a/store/search.cfm).

Another type of national standard can be found at the Mid-continent Research for Education and Learning (McREL) website (http://www .mcrel.org/compendium/browse.asp). Using the same format for all subject areas, and listing standards and topics for each area, the McREL standards are often used when a common format is needed (for example, *Information Power* refers to them when showing curriculum connections). Additionally, states have used these same concepts when developing their standards.

Less well known is the Partnership for 21st Century Skills, which is an alliance of educators, business, and policy leaders (the American Association of School Librarians is a partner) to define these skills, incorporate them into the curriculum, and assess to what extent they are being learned. So far North Carolina and West Virginia are developing twenty-first-century learning plans for their students. For more information, go to http://www.21stcenturyskills.org. (Note that outside the LMC environment, *information literacy* is called *information communication technology*, or ICT.)

State Standards

Even if your state does not have separate information literacy standards, these are undoubtedly inferred or addressed directly within the standards for the different subject areas. Since they are embedded in subject areas, you have another route for furthering collaboration with teachers. Show them how your teaching can help them cover these required skills and competencies.

There are two ways to find your state standards. You can either search your state's website or you can return to the Education World website (see the URL given above), where you start with the subject area. You then get a list of the states and can find what their individual standards are for that discipline. The latter approach is particularly helpful if you want to compare requirements among the states. Some state library associations also have links on their web pages and may also show how the SLMP connects to those standards.

Upholding Standards

Compare the McREL standards for a subject area with those of its national association. Which format do you prefer?

_____

Where does information literacy fit within your state's language arts, social studies, and science standards?

_____

With what other subject areas can you make a connection?

_____

NO CHILD LEFT BEHIND

Signed into law in January 2002, the No Child Left Behind Act (NCLB) has fundamentally affected education today. This legislation uses tests as the basis for determining whether schools are making "adequate yearly progress" (AYP). These tests are given every year to grades 3 through 8 in reading and math, and at least once to grades 10 through 12. In addition, science must be tested once within grades 3 to 5, 6 to 9, and 10 to 12. Students with limited English proficiency are tested for oral language, reading, and writing in English.

States are required to define AYP in terms of how much improvement should be expected over two years based on the lowest achieving group. This bar must be raised at least every three years so that at the end of twelve years of schooling, all students have attained the proficient level on reading/language arts and math tests. Schools that fail to make AYP over two years are defined as "needing improvement" and must offer tutoring services from a state-approved provider to low-income parents or provide transportation to a better public school. Further steps are taken if the AYP is not met in subsequent years until, after five years, the school must restructure, possibly reopening as a charter school, replacing the staff, or turning the school over to the state or a private operator.

School districts are expected to employ "highly qualified teachers," who are defined as holding a minimum of a bachelor's degree, having a full state license or certification, and demonstrating competence in the subject area in which they teach. For the latter, new elementary school teachers must pass a rigorous state test of their knowledge and ability to teach reading, writing, math, and other subjects in the curriculum. New middle and high school teachers, in addition to the test, must have majored (or taken the equivalent course work) in the subject they are teaching. For more detailed information see the U.S. Department of Education website (http://www.ed.gov) and click on "No Child Left Behind."

No Child Left Behind affects you in several ways. School districts and teachers' unions have opposed many aspects of the act, seeing it as inhibiting rather than promoting education. Although it no longer tracks the latest news, the NCLBGrassroots.org website has compiled information that shows how NCLB is failing students. Apart from the complaints from educators, you are affected by the "highly qualified" designation. While teacher associations do not like the stringency of the designation, SLMSs are upset that in most places they are not required to be "highly qualified." By implication, this suggests that they are not as important in education as teachers. The unions, which are fighting the designation, are not supportive of SLMSs being included within it. However, the AASL, working with the ALA Washington Office, has taken up the challenge and seeks to have SLMSs listed as "highly qualified," although it recognizes that the best outcome would be the elimination of that qualification for everyone.

Another serious impact of NCLB has been the reduction of funding available for LMC materials and the reduction of staff in LMCs. Since

NCLB is not funded by the government, states and local districts must cover the costs. A school "needing improvement" has to find a way to pay for tutoring. Even if AYP is achieved, testing is expensive. When making choices as to where the limited remaining money should be spent, districts choose classroom teachers over SLMSs (and definitely over funding the LMC) so that students will do well on the tests—despite all the replicated research showing that student achievement on these high-stakes tests directly correlates to an active SLMP with a strong collection.

At the elementary level, already-small SLMP budgets are being cut still further because of the advent of classroom collections. With the push for higher scores on reading tests and another government mandate, "Reading First," many districts are setting up book collections in every class. The funds to do this invariably come from what had previously been given to the SLMP.

Faced with the effects of a powerful national agenda, is there anything you can do? Advocacy is a key factor. Be sure to bring the latest research results to the attention of your administrator. If you have not done so as yet, download the research foundation paper "School Libraries Work!" (2006 ed.) from Scholastic Library Publishing (http://www.scholastic.com/librarians/printables/downloads/slw_2006.pdf) and give a copy to your administrator. Know what is tested and show how you, too, are teaching and reinforcing the skills students need. Find out what your association is doing to advocate for you with legislators and the department of education in your state. Stay informed and be the one who keeps others current with the latest edicts from the federal government. While there are no guarantees, you can position the SLMP so that it is regarded as a vital component of the school.

Avoiding Being Left Behind

What aspects of NCLB upset educators?

_____

Has your budget been affected by NCLB? (See if you can get pre-2002 figures for comparisons.)

_____

What is the difference between a classroom collection and a library?

_____

In what ways can the LMC be more directly involved with books for the classroom?

_____

Key Ideas

- As a professional you are expected to adhere to a code of ethics.

- Intellectual freedom in all its manifestations is fundamental to librarianship.

- Selection decisions are not an excuse for censorship.

- Students have a right to privacy concerning their choices in reading (and viewing).

- Implement the information literacy standards from both *Information Power* and NETS-S in your instruction.

- Fair use is frequently misused in schools.

- Preventing plagiarism requires education and collaboration with teachers.

- Know how to find national and state standards for all subject areas and be prepared to teach to them.

- Be familiar with NCLB and look for ways to minimize its negative impact on the SLMP.

NOTES

1. "Code of Ethics of the American Library Association," American Library Association, http://www.ala.org/ala/oif/statementspols/codeofethics/codeethics.htm.
2. "Library Bill of Rights," American Library Association, http://www.ala.org/ala/oif/statementspols/statementsif/librarybillrights.htm.
3. "Access to Resources and Services in the School Library Media Program: An Interpretation of the Library Bill of Rights," American Library Association, http://www.ala.org/ala/oif/statementspols/statementsif/interpretations/librarymediaprogram.pdf.
4. *Intellectual Freedom Manual,* 7th ed., compiled by Office for Intellectual Freedom (Chicago: American Library Association, 2006).
5. Theresa Chmara, "Minors' First Amendment Rights to Access Information," in *Intellectual Freedom Manual,* 384–93.
6. "Privacy Issues in K–12 School Library Media Centers," in *Privacy in the 21st Century: Issues for Public, School, and Academic Libraries,* by Helen R. Adams et al. (Westport, CT: Libraries Unlimited, 2005), 101–36.
7. "Information Literacy Standards for Student Learning," in *Information Power: Building Partnerships for Learning,* by American Association of School Librarians, Association for Educational Communications and Technology (Chicago: American Library Association, 1998), 8–9.
8. "Learning and Teaching," in *Information Power,* 58–82.
9. "Information Access and Delivery," in *Information Power,* 83–99.
10. "Curriculum and Content Area Standards—NETS for Students: Technology Foundation Standards for All Students," ISTE NETS Project, http://cnets.iste.org/currstands/cstands-netss.html.
11. "Copyright and Fair Use in the Classroom, on the Internet, and the World Wide Web," University of Maryland University College, http://www.umuc.edu/library/copy.html#whatis.

CHAPTER 12

Looking Back, Looking Forward

Well, I gained a lot of knowledge . . . but I still have lots to learn.

W ith the school year drawing to a close, you are probably feeling a mixture of exhaustion and exhilaration. If you had not known it before, you now are well aware that being a school library media specialist is a demanding job. However, you have survived and most likely managed to do a few things very successfully.

Before you begin assessing your first year, there are still some hurdles to overcome. Not surprisingly, what is still facing you is more complex than the classroom routine of posting grades, collecting textbooks, and saying good-bye to the class. You must close the library media center while still meeting the needs of teachers and students. After that you can focus on what comes next.

BRINGING THE YEAR TO A CLOSE

Sometimes it seems that you have to fit eight weeks of work into the final month of school in order to complete everything. With input from your principal, you must decide when to stop circulating material and whether or not to do an inventory. In addition, you need to handle issues relating to lost and overdue books, as well as end-of-the-year reports and final cleanup.

Closing Circulation

You customarily need an official date when all materials are due back in the LMC. Before you set it, discuss a reasonable cutoff point with your supervisor. Most likely you will be required to follow whatever the past practice was. In some places, particularly if you have a rigid schedule, you are expected to keep the LMC open until the last day of school. In that situation, you will probably have to put in several extra days—whether or not you are paid for them—to complete the procedures. If you have developed a good relationship with your principal, you might discuss the possibility of including compensation for this additional time in a future budget.

Even if you are allowed two weeks to finish the process, accept that the closing date is more a guideline than a hard-and-fast deadline. As soon as the date is announced, middle and high school students will approach you in a high state of alarm. They are behind on getting papers done, and although they can do all the online searches without a problem, their teacher is requiring them to include books in their "works cited" page, and they absolutely need more time. To address these problems and be sure your records are accurate, have them return the books by the closing date, and then *recheck them out*. At least you know they have the titles in their possession.

Teachers are equally concerned. Ask them to please return what they are no longer using and confirm that they have the books your records indicate are checked out to them. In elementary schools, and many secondary ones as well, where teachers have checked out a sizable collection of library books to use in the classroom, some of these titles disappear because students have taken them home, where they have inadvertently found a new resting place at the bottom of a closet or under a stack of other materials. Concerned teachers will make every effort to round up the missing items and will hopefully find them all, but you should, if at all possible, consider these losses as the cost of doing business. Think about which scenario you prefer—having teachers regularly choose fifty to one hundred books to circulate in the classroom or not having them check out any because of the fear that some will get lost.

In your zeal to complete the year in an orderly fashion, you cannot forget your philosophy or mission. Your LMC is an integral part of the school curriculum and as such, it cannot fully close before the rest of the school. Whether students or teachers are involved, you must be prepared to make adjustments to meet their needs.

Consider the possibility of summer loans. If you cannot do this for students, it is still a distinct help for teachers and is a simple matter for LMCs that are not automated. If your LMC is automated, call your tech support and find out how to allow it.

Equipment Return

If, as is typical, you are responsible for distributing equipment at the start of the school year, it is also your job to collect everything at the end, as well as clean and check it for needed repairs. This is one task that has become somewhat simpler over the years, since there are fewer overhead and filmstrip (some schools still have them) projectors. Probably no one has to deal with 16-mm projectors any more.

Prepare a checklist for each type of equipment. List their assigned numbers. Schedule the smallest items to be returned first so that the larger ones do not clutter the LMC too soon. Clean and check operations on everything you have on hand. You can do simple repairs and lamp changes yourself (or train a volunteer or your clerk). Note how many lamps you have remaining. You may need to order more to cover requirements for the next school year.

Expect that some teachers will speak to you about keeping their equipment beyond the date for which you have requested its return. Offer to exchange what they have with something you have already checked and cleaned, and allow them to keep it until the next-to-last day of school. When they turn it in, all you do is check that it is back.

If you have not had to do so earlier in the year, ask what the procedures are for sending equipment out for repair. Note the problems with the equipment on your checklist as well as on the repair tag. Before giving these items out next year, you will have to make sure the problem was fixed.

Organized Closing

When was circulation closed last year?

_____

If you have a library management system, how do you set the date for closing circulation?

_____

For how many types of equipment are you responsible?

_____

INVENTORY

Whether you are doing an automated or a paper inventory, you will need as many extra volunteers as you can get. Set up a schedule and have the volunteers fill in their days and time on it, along with a telephone number so you can reach them if necessary. Even if your LMC is automated, the first task is to put the shelves in exact order. While you can scan bar codes in any sequence, and many library management systems will let you know if a book is in the wrong location, you have to check the shelves when students claim they returned something and you show it is still missing.

Both types of inventory can get started even when books are still being checked out, but it is far simpler with an automated system, since you can do one at any time during the year. Begin with reference, since none of that collection circulates, and move on to areas that have low demand so as to minimize inventoried items being borrowed. Maintain daily records of which sections have been done (and by whom) so that you know if a returned book is to be shelved in an inventoried area. In that case, you must either scan the bar code in or check the shelf list.

Automated Systems

Read your manual on initiating the inventory process. Even if you are sure you understand what to do, call tech support and have them walk you through the steps. Find out what types of reports can be generated and decide which ones you want.

The speed at which the job can be completed depends on the number of volunteers and scanners you have. If there is only one scanner on hand, it will take a long time, since each book must be physically handled. Ask other SLMSs in your district if they are doing an inventory. Some schools conduct them every two or three years, so they might be able to lend you theirs, or if your collections are not very large, you might be able to share scanners by staggering the days that you do inventory.

Consider running some interim printouts of sections that have been scanned. You can then check to see if any books listed as missing are on the shelves. Some of your helpers may be skipping titles or not using the equipment properly. Another possibility is that some step was overlooked in the inventory procedure. You want to identify problems as early as possible so that you can fix them.

Be sure you know how to conclude an inventory. Once again, reading the manual is important, but you should also talk with tech support. In the future, you may be comfortable without the telephone help, but for your first one you want to be sure that you have not overlooked something. Take some time to analyze the reports to see what might be communicated to your administrator to demonstrate the needs or strengths of your collection and the SLMP.

Paper Systems

If your LMC is not automated (and there are still many that are not), you can use a small army of volunteers. Have them work in pairs, with one holding the appropriate shelf list drawer and the other checking the books. Instruct them to turn inventoried titles horizontally with spines facing up. If a book is missing, the shelf list card is either turned on its side so it sticks up or a clip is put on it. (Clips are neater, but they can slip off, or two or more cards can be inadvertently attached to each other.)

In cases where there are several copies of the same title, volunteers must be sure that all are on hand using the information on the shelf list card (copy or accession number). To identify missing copies, the number is checked *in pencil* and the card is clipped or placed on its side. If the book shows up, the mark is erased. Once all the books on the card are back, it is turned down to its normal position or the clip is removed.

Alert volunteers to the possibility of finding books that were previously marked as lost on the shelf list card. These have a way of reappearing after a year or two. Have them erase the penciled note and proceed as they would with any other book that is in its proper place.

After a bookcase has been inventoried, you will see that most books are turned down but one or two are still standing. The upright titles are ones for which there are no shelf list cards. Check first to be sure the book has not been misshelved. If it is where it belongs, it is probably a title that had been lost for several years and the shelf list card was destroyed. Either you or a responsible volunteer should create a temporary one on a colored 3 × 5 card with the necessary information. Place it standing up in the drawer for a later step.

When the inventory is complete, go through the cards that are standing and do a final check to be sure the books are not on the shelf. Then note in pencil that the title (or copy when appropriate) is lost, add the date (e.g., lost 6/06), and take off the clip. For those with notes and dates that indicate they have been lost for two or more years, remove and discard the shelf list card.

Remove the colored cards. Type and file new ones. The final task is to turn all the books upright. For once the shelves look beautiful, with all spines coming to the edge.

Anticipating Inventory

How many people will there be to help you do inventory?

_____

After doing the reference collection, in what sequence will you do the remainder of the inventory?

_____

For automated inventories, how many scanners will you have?

_____

For paper inventories, which of your volunteers are experienced with this procedure?

_____

OVERDUE AND LOST MATERIALS

Look for paperwork on overdue and lost books from the previous year. It is helpful to have copies of letters sent home about missing items so that you know how these are worded. Many library management systems have report templates that you can run. Check your manual to see what is available.

In sending overdue notices to classes, be mindful of students' privacy. Do not simply put the lists in teachers' boxes. Use sealed envelopes with the students' names on the outside.

See if you are expected to send the office a list of materials not returned by the end of school, so that secretaries can collect anything turned in during the vacation period. Is there a procedure or form that you are expected to complete so that they know how much is owed, or do you just create the list and turn it in to them on the last day of school?

Find out what penalties the school imposes on students who have not returned books. Some places withhold report cards; others do not send next year's schedule until all obligations are cleared. If you charge fines (not all LMCs do), is there a limit? Have amnesty days been scheduled in the past? If so, you probably should continue them because students will wait for this to avoid large fines—which is one reason why many LMCs have discontinued the practice.

How do you charge for lost materials? Do you add the fine to the original cost? Do you discount for age? For example, you might have a limit of five dollars for anything over twenty years old, since you certainly will not be replacing it. Give receipts (and keep copies) to anyone who pays for lost material. State on it the time limit for getting a refund if the item is found. You usually have to turn in the money you collected. If someone wants a refund in the fall, you will not have the cash to give them.

Be prepared for complaints. Parents and students will assure you that they returned the items long ago or never checked them out in the first place. Do not lose your patience. Allow them to check the shelves, or go with them, to verify that the material is not in the LMC. Once that has been established, calmly let them know your records indicate that they are the ones who charged out those books, and according to the rules, they are responsible. Some may go to the principal and complain. If you are overruled, be gracious and comment that while you had to follow procedures, administrators can make allowances in special cases and you are glad they found a way to resolve it.

In addition to students losing materials, teachers often cannot locate what they have checked out during the year. Districts vary as to whether or not you charge faculty for lost items. If you have a choice, do *not* impose any fees. As previously discussed, there are many ways in which these materials might have disappeared—and they frequently are the ones that turn up after a while. Asking your colleagues to pay, even if it is school policy, can have a negative impact on your relationship with them. Avoid it as much as possible.

Among the Missing

What policies does your school have regarding lost materials?

_____

What would you say to a parent who claimed her child had returned everything and suggested your records were wrong?

_____

How can you calm teachers who are upset at learning what items are still checked out to them?

_____

FINAL TASKS

Before you can take a well-deserved vacation, you need to complete a few more tasks that bring your program and facility to a proper close. First and foremost is to do an annual report, as described in chapter 7. Despite having accomplished a great deal in one year, remember not to ramble on in the report. Focus on the most significant achievements, identify a *few* problems you plan to address in the following year, and include as much numerical data as possible to showcase the SLMP. If you have built a positive relationship with your principal, find out when you can drop in for an informal discussion during the summer.

Typically, you will get a packet of papers detailing items that need to be completed in order for you to officially check out. Go through them carefully and ask questions if you are not sure of anything. Observe all deadlines. If there are any tasks you can finish early, do so, since you need to get signatures indicating that you have done them and lines develop as the last day approaches.

You probably have to sign off that teachers have returned all items to the LMC. As noted earlier, this can be tricky. If necessary, you can sign out items for the summer to give them more time to locate anything that is missing.

Whether or not you are paid for it, plan on coming in during vacation. If you do not, you will be greeted when you come back with a mountain of mail to sift through, possible problems with orders that you could have straightened out before school began, and boxes everywhere. Putting in a few hours several times during the summer will let you return ready to work with students and teachers, rather than facing a multitude of back room tasks for which you will have no time.

Most SLMSs find themselves so busy during the year that papers and books pile up on their desk. Now is the time to clear things away, file what is important, and toss the rest. Although it is technically the job of custodians, you might literally clean your desk and computer screen. While cleaning, go through your computer documents as well and see what can be deleted. Create an archive file for items you are unwilling to eliminate but will clutter the files you use on a daily basis.

Walls are next. Remove posters from walls and take down bulletin boards. In some districts this is required as part of summer cleanup. Look at the LMC with a critical eye. Is there anything that needs repair (for example, leaky windows or stained ceiling tiles) or cleaning (such as carpets or lounge chairs)? Even if you have not been given a form for recording these, make a list and submit it. Check to see if you have to prepare work orders to get things done.

Finally, walk along the shelves and see that all books are standing upright, with spines at the edge of the shelves and bookends in place. Make a note of any overly tight shelves. The section will either have to be weeded or you will need to shift the books to make room for new titles. With everything in order, you can confidently leave the LMC knowing that it will be ready to welcome students and teachers when classes resume.

Closing Down the LMC

What three accomplishments will you highlight in your annual report?

_____

What one problem will you bring to your administrator's attention?

_____

What do you already know needs to be cleaned or repaired?

_____

SELF-ASSESSMENT

Before you get too relaxed, take time to look at what occurred over the school year. What worked and what did not? How did the job measure up to the expectations you had when you accepted it? Were there any surprises?

Look at all your responsibilities and reflect first on your successes. Go through the chapters in this book to remind yourself of what you were attempting to accomplish. Pat yourself on the back as you see how much you learned and what you were able to achieve. Developing— or even maintaining—an active SLMP and the tasks that support it, from ordering materials to building relationships with everyone in the educational community, is a complex and demanding job.

How well did your philosophy and vision work in guiding your actions? Are there any changes you would want to make to either of them? While your philosophy and vision should be fairly constant, you might find that the experiences of your first year on the job have given you new insights.

Of course, there will be places where you made mistakes. You might have mishandled a teacher complaint or lost patience with students. While acknowledging these missteps, let yourself off the hook. No one is perfect, not even very experienced SLMSs.

Looking at both the positives and negatives, note your strengths. You will build on them next year. Identify where you are most challenged. Look for courses or workshops that will help you deal with these areas. Accept the fact that there will always be areas in which you can learn and grow.

How Did You Do?

Where were you most successful? Why?

_____

What challenged you? Why?

_____

Where will you go for help?

_____

PROFESSIONAL GROWTH

While your school district provides in-service days or staff development workshops, you probably have found that these rarely relate to what you do each day. If you want to grow professionally, you will need to seek out opportunities on your own. You want your students to become lifelong learners; model the practice yourself.

Conferences and Courses

Those of you who just completed library school may not want to return to the classroom, but you should check to see what professional development courses are offered. Many these days are available online and are the best way to keep current. With rapid changes in information technology and new trends in education affecting what you do, you cannot afford to coast on the courses you have completed. You will be outdated before you know it.

School districts tend to pay for a certain number of courses in a given year. Find out what yours offers and the procedures to file for this benefit. In addition to obtaining the knowledge you need, after accruing a certain number of credits you are generally eligible for a pay increase.

Numerous national conferences take place each year, with presentations by people who are leaders in their field, as well as exhibits that will give you ideas for what you want to have in your LMC. Although many of these conferences are scheduled while school is in session, making it difficult for you to attend, most of you will have no problem with the ALA's Annual Conference, which occurs in late June. Check the website of the AASL (http://www.ala.org/aasl/) for scholarship awards that defray the cost of going to a conference. Some state associations offer these as well.

State library associations also tend to put on annual conferences. If you cannot go to a national one, try your best to get to these. Since they usually occur over a weekend (with additional days alongside), even if you are not given time off you can probably be there for at least part of the conference. The chance to network with colleagues is as rewarding and educational as going to a workshop.

Professional Associations

To be regarded as a professional, you need to behave like one. Being a member of your state library association is a bare beginning. Go one step up by volunteering for a committee so that you can begin learning about new aspects of your job.

Those who truly want to be exemplary join national organizations. The American Library Association is the largest and most important of these, representing all types of libraries. Within its structure are various divisions, the one most relevant to you being the American Association of School Librarians. The size of the ALA gives it clout in Washington, D.C., and provides a vast array of services and programs for members. Throughout this book we have mentioned a number of these resources provided by and through the ALA. Do not let the dues be an obstacle. If you divided the cost by the number of weeks in a year, it is about what you pay for one gallon of gas, and look at what you get in return!

Both the ALA and AASL publish journals that focus on issues of significant interest to you. Obviously, if you volunteer for a committee you will learn even more. Although the best way to serve on a committee is to be a face-to-face member and attend both the Midwinter and Annual conferences, since much of the work is conducted via e-mail, many committees now allow virtual members.

In addition to the ALA and AASL, you might consider other divisions of the ALA such as the Association for Library Service to Children, which gives out the Newbery and Caldecott Awards, or the Young Adult Library Services Association. Other national associations include the Association for Educational Communications and Technology and the International Society for Technology in Education, which is responsible for the National Educational Technology Standards.

National Board for Professional Teaching Standards

If you really want to demonstrate your professionalism, after a few years on the job consider becoming a National Board Certified Teacher. As Gail Dickinson observes in the introduction to her book on how to go about it, the process "has been described as rigorous, intense, fulfilling, and the best professional growth experience one could ever have."[1]

The requirements are extensive, and documenting that you have mastered them takes months. Not everyone who goes through the process gets certified, so if you undertake it, do it conscientiously. There are no shortcuts. Gail Dickinson's book is a vital tool, but you will also want to talk to those in your state who have been certified. Look at their portfolio to get an idea of what it entails.

When you are ready to investigate this, see what help your state association offers to candidates. In addition to connecting you with those who are certified, some associations offer scholarships to offset the costs. There is also a Candidate Subsidy Program made possible by the U.S. Department of Education. For more information, go to http://www.nbpts.org.

A Larger Perspective

Is there a conference you plan to attend or a course you want to take?

_____

To what professional associations do you currently belong?

_____

Which professional associations do you plan to join?

_____

KEEPING YOUR ENTHUSIASM HIGH

One last bit of reflection. Being successful as an SLMS depends heavily on your personality and attitude. In one school the SLMS remarked to her new assistant, "If you give teachers what they want, they will only come back for more." It is hard to argue with that, but you can already tell that she had a dead SLMP.

While that is an extreme example, the daily demands can drain your energy and make you irritable. When you allow the negatives to overwhelm your passion for what you do, your program will suffer.

To avoid the effects of stress and its potential for causing you to burn out, remember the following:

- Set realistic goals
- Prioritize
- Don't procrastinate
- Get advice or help
- Find the fun
- Know your calming techniques
- Get another "job"

Putting too many items on your "to-do" list only makes you frustrated and overwhelmed. Be sure you know what is most important. (It is not always what *you* think should be done first, since an administrator's request or demand automatically gets top priority.) Avoiding the jobs you do not like only make them weigh more heavily on you. Asking for help is a sign of wisdom, not weakness. Look for a mentor and develop relationships with the other SLMSs in your district. When days seem to spin out of control, laugh at the absurdity of it. What you do is important, but it is not life or death; do not take it too seriously. Know what activities and behaviors calm you down and build them into your schedule, whether they are walks, bubble baths, or reading mysteries. The last suggestion on the list does not mean for you to quit what you are doing, but rather to get a hobby, or better yet, volunteer your time in some worthy organization. Do not let your work become the center of your life.

So we have finally come to the end. Congratulate yourself on having successfully completed your first year on the job. Celebrate having a profession that allows you to make a difference in the lives of others, and look forward to growing further so that you can do even more for the students and teachers in your school.

Staying Passionate

What signs let you know that you are becoming stressed?

_____

To whom do you turn for advice?

_____

What is your favorite way of reducing stress, and how often do you use it?

_____

Key Ideas

- Keep the date for closing circulation flexible to meet the needs of teachers and students.
- Find out what your responsibilities are for equipment return and repair.
- Solicit volunteers and set up a schedule in advance of inventorying.
- Start your inventory with the least-used sections of the collection.
- Ask secretaries if a form is used to list students and the items they still owe the LMC.
- Learn the policy for billing students and teachers for lost materials.
- Prepare a brief annual report with numerous statistics and highlights of achievements.
- Plan to drop in to the LMC over the summer.
- Know what needs to be cleaned or repaired.
- Honest self-assessment prepares you for the next school year.
- Look for opportunities to grow as a professional.
- Know what you need to do to maintain your passion.

NOTE

1. Gail Dickinson, *Achieving National Board Certification for School Library Media Specialists: A Study Guide* (Chicago: American Library Association, 2006), xi.

Essential Resources

In addition to *New on the Job,* you should be familiar with the following titles and have them on your professional shelf. Bookmark the websites for ready access.

Adams, Helen R., et al. *Privacy in the 21st Century: Issues for Public, School, and Academic Libraries.* Westport, CT: Libraries Unlimited, 2005.

This comprehensive exploration of all aspects of privacy, including federal and state laws, is a necessary title in a world that is both litigious and reacting to terrorism.

American Association of School Librarians, Association for Educational Communications and Technology. *Information Power: Building Partnerships for Learning.* Chicago: American Library Association, 1998.

The fourth edition since 1960 (with a new version in the planning stages), this core document focuses on standards and guidelines for the school library profession as they affect teaching and learning, information access, and program administration. Keep any earlier versions of this book to see the evolution as well as constants in its standards for the profession.

American Library Association. http://www.ala.org.

In addition to the home page of this organization, you should bookmark the sites for the American Association of School Librarians (http://www.ala.org/aasl/) and the Office for Intellectual Freedom (http://www.ala.org/oif/; telephone 800-545-2433; fax 312-280-4227).

Association for Supervision and Curriculum Development. http://www.ascd.org.

Keep abreast of the latest trends in education and speak knowledgeably with administrators by checking this website.

Crews, Kenneth. *Copyright Law for Librarians and Educators: Creative Strategies and Practical Solutions.* Chicago: American Library Association, 2005.

This guide covers all the basics of copyright law, from regulations on text to those for digital information, as well as clarifying the concept of fair use. An equally good choice is Carrie Russell, *Complete Copyright: An Everyday Guide for Librarians* (Chicago: American Library Association, 2004).

eSchoolNews Online. http://www .eschoolnews.org.

This website has daily updates on almost everything relating to technology in education, and it also has resource centers dealing with solutions to current challenges.

MarcoPolo Internet Content for the Classroom. http://www.marcopolo -education.org.

With this rapidly growing resource, you can find a variety of projects for use with teachers across the curriculum. Check the links to its educational partner sites.

National Educational Technology Standards. http://www.iste.org/nets/.

Find the standards for students, teachers, and administrators, along with resources to build them into the curriculum, on the website of the International Society for Technology in Education.

No Child Left Behind. http://www.ed.gov/ nclb/.

Current and historical information is available here on all aspects of the law that has changed the face of American education.

Office for Intellectual Freedom. *Intellectual Freedom Manual.* 7th ed. Chicago: American Library Association, 2005.

This book is an excellent source for understanding the implications of all aspects of censorship and intellectual freedom. It includes the Library Bill of Rights, the Code of Ethics, policy state-ments, and guidelines.

The School Librarian's Workshop. Berkeley Heights, NJ: Library Learning Resources, 1980–.

This is a bimonthly 24-page newsletter edited by the authors of *New on the Job.* It provides K–12 SLMSs with teaching units, professional development, tech-nology updates, children's literature, bulletin board ideas, and ready-to-use activities. See also http://www.school

Jobbers and Vendors

This list is not meant to be comprehensive. It is for your reference if you are the first SLMS the school has had or if you are looking for some alternatives when the service you are getting from your current vendor does not meet your expectations. Some of the companies listed here cover multiple areas; for example, EBSCO is both a periodical jobber and an online subscription vendor.

Book Jobbers

Baker and Taylor, Inc.
800-775-1800
http://www.btol.com

Brodart Co.
800-233-8467
http://www.brodart.com

Follett Library Resources
888-511-5114
http://www.flr.follett.com

Periodical Jobbers

EBSCO Information Services
205-991-6600
http://www.ebsco.com

W. T. Cox Subscriptions
800-571-9554
http://www.wtcox.com

Library Supply Houses

Demco, Inc.
800-279-1586
http://www.demco.com

Gaylord Brothers
800-448-6160
http://www.gaylord.com

Highsmith, Inc.
800-558-2110
http://www.highsmith.com

Online Databases and Encyclopedias

ABC-CLIO
800-968-1911
http://www.abc-clio.com

Encyclopaedia Britannica
800-621-3900
http://www.eb.com

Grolier Online
(Scholastic Publishing Company)
800-621-1115
http://www.scholastic.com/
   librarypublishing/

H. W. Wilson
800-367-6770
http://www.hwwilson.com

Thomson Gale
800-877-4253
http://www.gale.com

World Book Inc.
800-344-3482
http://www.worldbook.com

Automation Systems

Alexandria/Companion Corp.
800-347-6439
http://www.companioncorp.com

Brodart Co.
800-233-8467
http://www.brodart.com

Follett Software Company
800-323-3397
http://www.fsc.follett.com

TLC
800-325-7759
http://www.TLCdelivers.com

Open Source Automation Systems

Koha
http://www.koha.org

OPALS
http://www.opals-na.org

GLOSSARY

This glossary of frequently used terms, many of which appear in this book, is far from complete. When you hear references to terms you do not understand, ask colleagues for help. For a very complete list of educational terminology, see "A Lexicon for Learning" at the website of the Association for Supervision and Curriculum Development (go to http://www.ascd.org and enter "lexicon" in the search box).

automation—*see* library management system

call number—classification (Dewey Decimal number) and letters of author's last name that indicate where a book is shelved; found on the book's spine label and on the card or record in the catalog

CEU (continuing education units)—credits awarded for attendance at extended workshops that can be accrued toward advancing to a higher level on the salary guide

differentiated instruction—teaching organized so that students of varying ability levels are equally challenged by the tasks they are to do

duty period—a non-teaching assignment such as bus or hall duty

encumbered—money set aside from your budget to pay for items on order

fixed schedule—*see* rigid schedule

flexible schedule—a schedule developed on an as-needed basis in response to teacher requests and curricular requirements. Teachers generally accompany their students to the LMC and participate in the lessons there.

graphic organizer—any of various designs to help students keep track of ideas and see their relationship; also known as mind or concept mapping

IEP (individualized education plan)—a right of students with special needs, generally designed by a team consisting of a special education teacher, a classroom teacher, a building principal, a psychologist, and the child's parents or guardians, to create the optimum teaching methods and best learning environment for the child. SLMSs need to check the IEP for students they see regularly.

ISBN (International Standard Book Number)—a unique ten- or thirteen-digit code to identify a book, helpful for ordering titles digitally and ensuring that the exact title and format are received

ISSN (International Standard Serial Number)—a unique 8-digit number that identifies journals and magazines and other serials

jobber—a vendor that supplies books or magazines from a number of different publishers

library management system—a computer- or web-based system incorporating the OPAC (catalog), circulation and cataloging of library materials, and a report-generating system to prepare overdue notices and conduct an inventory

PO (purchase order)—a form used by school districts for all acquisitions; always includes the vendor, items to be purchased, their cost, and the budget line from which it is to be paid

prep period (or prep time)—a contractual preparation period for teachers to complete work necessary for their classes, including making copies, calling parents, or just down time

RFP (request for proposal)—a compilation of what you are looking for (usually in a library automation system) that is sent out to a number of vendors so you can recommend to the school board the one that comes closest to your criteria

rigid schedule—a schedule defined by assigned blocks of time for classes to come to the LMC for instruction and book selection and return, allowing teachers, who drop students at the door and leave, to have their contractual prep period

rubric—a means of objectifying a subjective analysis, such as the grade for a student project, by indicating what constitutes poor, good, and excellent levels for each of the assignment's components

shelf shifting—moving books from one shelf to another to even out the space and avoid overcrowding, usually affecting numerous shelves in order to achieve the desired look

specials—non-classroom teachers such as those for art, music, physical education, and SLMSs who follow a rigid schedule, creating free time for teachers' prep periods

weeding—removing material that is outdated or too battered to remain in the collection

INDEX

INDEX

Ruth Toor is a library media consultant, having retired after 29 years as a school library media specialist at the elementary school level in Chatham, New Jersey. She is a past president of the AASL, a past member of the ALA Council, and still works actively on ALA, AASL, and ALSC committees. She is also a past president of the Educational Media Association of New Jersey (now the New Jersey Association of School Librarians). Toor is currently the Internship Adviser for Professional Development Studies at Rutgers SCILS, the School of Communication, Information and Library Studies. She earned her B.A. at the University of Delaware and her M.L.S. at Rutgers SCILS.

Hilda K. Weisburg is a library media consultant who recently retired after 31 years as a school library media specialist at high school and elementary levels in Sayreville and Morristown, New Jersey. She is a past president of the Educational Media Association of New Jersey and is the association's delegate to the AASL's Affiliate Assembly, currently serving as Region II director. She has served on numerous AASL committees and has chaired a number of them. Weisburg has also taught graduate courses as an adjunct at Rutgers SCILS and has served as a consultant for several New Jersey districts. She earned her B.S. from Montclair State University and her M.L.S. from Columbia University.

Together Toor and Weisburg have written 11 professional books and write and edit *The School Librarian's Workshop,* currently in its 27th year of publication, and read by SLMSs in the United States, Canada, and 25 other countries. They have offered presentations at AASL and state library media conferences and have given staff development workshops for many school districts.